Malcolm,

In my opinion, you are a
star already!
— Best personal regards.

HOW
TO MEET
THE PRESS

Jack Hilton

HOW
TO MEET
THE PRESS

A Survival Guide

DODD, MEAD & COMPANY
NEW YORK

Published by Dodd, Mead & Company, Inc.
71 Fifth Avenue, New York, New York 10003
Distributed in Canada by
McClelland and Stewart Limited, Toronto
Manufactured in the United States of America
Designed by Karen Fortgang
First Edition

1 2 3 4 5 6 7 8 9 10

Library of Congress Cataloging-in-Publication Data

Hilton, Jack, 1937–
How to meet the press

Includes index.
1. Public speaking. 2. Press conferences
I. Title.
PN4193.P73H54   1987   808.53   86-32968
ISBN 0-396-08914-3

For My Dad

Contents

Contents

ACKNOWLEDGMENTS

It happened gradually and almost imperceptibly to me. The process is called attrition; it decidedly wasn't on purpose or deliberate. But a number of years ago I completed the transformation from a night person to the diametric opposite of same; now my eyelids roll back revealing light (if any) at approximately 5 A.M. This happens, with or without the intrusion of an alarm clock, usually seven mornings per week. Mondays through Fridays I hasten to my office in Manhattan, arriving with a smattering of similarly afflicted type-A people at 7:15, the commuter railroad permitting.

On Saturdays and Sundays it's different. I creep to the kitchen, brew coffee in the largest urn available, and write. Early morning hours are the best for me, mostly owing to the absence of distractions and interruptions. This book is the product of 150 of those Saturdays and Sundays, some more productive than others. (One hundred fifty is a guess. I didn't keep a record.)

The above-mentioned transformation remains incomplete (or uncommenced) for the rest of my family, but they aren't sloths either; they, too, eventually rise. And because my reclusiveness on weekends sometimes perpetuates until mid-afternoon, the first of my thanks and acknowledgments are rightfully owed to them for keeping me undistracted and uninterrupted for prolonged periods of time—which otherwise they might have claimed.

My inspiration and assistance as a media consultant have come over the years from a legion of persons whose names and faces come immediately to mind in a collage, including all of my colleagues and clients. Collectively, and in some cases, individually, I have learned far more from them than vice versa. Some of these names are big names, others are not so big to anyone but me. However I hesitate to undertake jotting them down for fear that somebody might be forgotten in a process that is now rushed as my publisher beckons. That would be inexcusable; also inevitable. So I won't start what I can't comprehensively finish unless Mr. Dodd and Mr. Mead will permit additions to the list (no subtractions, I promise) as they occur to me for an indeterminate time. Besides, my advisers and friends know who they are, and many of their names are included in context on the forthcoming pages.

Finally, I have outlasted three or four secretaries in the preparation of this manuscript (a process having started, it seems, shortly after the Inchon landing). I am exceedingly grateful to the current corps and the alumni association, now scattered elsewhere from Eighth Avenue in New York City to London, England. (The one in London did most of the last work under duress caused more by a harried publisher and editor than by me, and she got the farthest away.) Mostly cheerfully, although sometimes in a state of controlled exasperation, they kept typing and typing and typing these words until they (and I) finally got everything rite.

Jack Hilton
New Canaan, Connecticut

FOREWORD

Fred W. Friendly
Former President, CBS News;
Director, Columbia University
Seminars on Media and Society;

Edward R. Murrow Professor Emeritus;
Columbia University Graduate
School of Journalism

It isn't recorded how many Americans face the press annually, but it may be in the low millions, journalism having become a major light industry. Never before in history have we practiced so much of it. Some of it with rare diligence and intelligence, much of it with a penchant for police blotter headlines and two-headed calves, as Walter Lippmann once put it. Reporters with note pads or microphones and cameras are seemingly everywhere in search of their daily fodder—which often far transcends the strictest interpretations of the word *news*. Even in the absence of momentous occurrences, stories must be written and rewritten every day, columns must be filled, and programs on TV and radio must be produced and transmitted.

As the author of this book proclaims in a later chapter, it is truly a "cacophony." That's an apt description—to which I might add that your voice as a business executive or public official may someday be invited to join the chorus, no matter who you are or from whence you come, even if you are a publisher or a network mogul. If it happens, you would do well to read Jack Hilton's book. His previous works along these lines have been avidly consumed for many years by political figures and business leaders; men and women who are keenly aware how important it is to meet the press successfully and perhaps persuasively. The reader should have no doubts as to whence author Hilton comes. He is, by definition, a coach for those who fear, distrust or may just be properly wary of the investigative reporter in search of much malpractice or simply the inside story. It is an adversarial relationship and just as the journalist had his coaches, schools and texts, the business executive is entitled to a reading of his "Miranda Rights," although there is always a right to remain silent—the business boss in the midst of a crisis may do so at his own peril. Irving Shapiro when he was CEO at DuPont taught us all that silence is not always golden and that returning reporters' phone calls can be the best defense, even if your attorney frowns at the very idea. Even if you are not summoned by a persistent news hound, there are fascinating lessons and anecdotes to be gleaned from Jack's book about the media environment and economics in America, and how it all works (or sometimes doesn't). Don't curse it, the First Amendment was essential when Madison wrote it two centuries ago and still is.

We live in paradoxical times. Never before in the course of human history has more information been disseminated to more people in as many forms. Still no one can argue that never before have we had such a large populace that receives or retains so little. Notwithstanding intense coverage for several weeks, three-fifths of the persons surveyed in the 1986 poll didn't recognize William Rehnquist's name when he was nominated (after 14 years of service on the Supreme Court) to be Chief Justice, they claimed. Results such as those are not unprecedented or atypical. We may be living in the world's first age of *information pollution*.

Information whizzes past us from thousands of publications and broadcast sources 24 hours a day, seven days a week, 365 days a year. It's a never-ending stream of so-called hard news, gossip, soft news,

facts, quasi-facts, truths, half-truths, partial-truths, rumors, specula-
tions and impressions, etc. Keeping it straight is at least a chore, if not
impossible. We are tempted on occasion to raise our hands and say:
"Stop! I would like time to absorb some of this; to understand it
better."

It is no wonder that many Americans seem to be walking around in a
semi-catatonic state where nobody seems to know much about
anything, or can remember particular things from one day to the
next. The material seems to be pitched at the public like confetti in
the hope or expectation that the public's mind is like velcro and some
of it will stick. Who can remember whether they saw a particular
piece of information on the nightly local or networks news program,
the daily newspaper, or the cover of the *National Enquirer* as they
were checking out at a supermarket?

Information pollution has two aspects to it. One, as we have seen, is
the sheer volume. The second is what we might call the homogeniza-
tion of information. This is a more recent phenomenon where news
information is presented in such a way that it begins to resemble other
things. The result is an untidy blending of types and forms to the
point where it becomes difficult to distinguish between news,
entertainment and advertisements.

Whether it is true or not, our perception is that important information used to be clearly labeled as important information. History was
history, news was news, entertainment was entertainment, commercials were commercials. It may be true that there was entertainment
value in newspapers, such as the comic strips and human interest
stories, but you could still delineate between news and entertainment by purchasing newspapers that were more serious about the
presentation of information. Television has changed all that. Somewhere in the late 1960s, television news crossed a threshold, from
which in the media's ethos, there is no return—news became
profitable. Up until that time news and public affairs were considered
an obligation or something that stations and networks did to keep
their licenses—not a profit center. Because it was done to impress, it
was by and large, serious. In the early days of television, news was
almost totally presented and produced by serious, well-educated

people with extensive backgrounds in news. Most of them came to the American audiences having been tempered by newspaper or wire service experiences, and more often came out of the cauldron of World War II. The names are now legendary—Edward R. Murrow, Walter Cronkite, Alexander Kendrick, Howard K. Smith, Eric Sevareid, Charles Collingwood, etc.

The late 60s saw a change in television. While always conscious of the bottom line, the pressure on television to maximize profits escalated because of intense pressure from affiliated stations, shareholders, and that vague Eminence Grise, the barons of Wall Street. It was in this environment that television news (primarily at the local level) moved over that magic line. Someone figured out if you put more entertainment value into a news program, featured a certain type of anchorperson, shortened pieces, did more soft features, etc., a station could turn what had been an obligation into an extraordinary profitable part of its programming schedule. Once that line was passed, it became impossible not to apply all the other rules of television to the presentation of news. Inevitably we began to see the drive toward the lowest common denominator, the use of consultants to determine the right anchor combinations, the increased role of weather people, happy-talk among the news presenters—all in an effort to become the number one rated news program in the market.

For a while the phenomenon was restricted to local news. Over the past few years the disease has crept into network news as well. Multimillion dollar contracts for anchorpeople and reporters, softening of news, megabuck changes in the frills and peripheries of presentation like sets and studios, dependence on visual stories, etc., have led to a frenzied fight to dominate the ratings numbers.

Today when you pick up a newspaper, you will inevitably read stories about the scorecard. The same newspapers which scoff at the ratings game flash blazing headlines about which network has the fraction or a percentage point lead; who won the week's battle for number one amongst the three network news services, as if there really was any statistical difference between NBC having a 11.8 rating and CBS having an 11.6. On many of the programs it is almost impossible to determine where news ends and entertainment begins. *Good Morn-*

ing America is produced by the Entertainment Division of ABC with news inserts. The *Today Show* is produced by the News Division of NBC with, presumably, entertainment inserts. In 1986, CBS announced the demise of the *Morning News* after years of futile pursuit of their rivals because, among other reasons, they felt that audiences did not want anything in the morning that was billed as a news program.

Can anyone actually tell the programs apart? To a casual viewer they represent a carnival featuring entertainers, rock stars, movie actors, surrogate mothers, rapists and victims, and where, if you look hard enough, you might, just might, find some information that may prove useful to you as a citizen.

Television's identity crisis would be overwhelming if it only involved the fact that its news programs have begun to look like its entertainment programs. The problem becomes mind-boggling when the audience is also confronted by entertainment programs that are fiction, but purport to be about real-live events and people. Docudramas have always been problematic as an art form. However, until recently they had been restricted to historical events. The current spate of docudramas has increasingly concentrated on events that were headlines of recent memory, such as the Atlanta child murders. How can any viewer, except the most sophisticated, keep anything straight? Are they watching a news program or an entertainment program? Is this a documentary or fiction or a docudrama?

Abby Mann, who wrote the "Atlanta Child Murders," stated that, of course, there were elements of fiction in his program and that, of course, the program was slanted to a particular point-of-view, but isn't that what dramatic productions are all about? I imagine the answer is yes. But what about the poor viewer who has just watched a network present a news program and is now watching the same network present a docudrama about a news event that only recently appeared on the same news program? Is he or she informed that the material by definition is slanted, distorted and, most important—fiction? Even if informed, does everyone watching this mixture over a period of time have the capacity to make these types of subtle distinctions?

To top off all the confusion, television presents its information in a linear fashion where it is difficult for the mind to make shifts of orientation. A soap opera precedes a game show followed by the news program and another game show. Within the structure of a news program, information about the nuclear arms race and Chief Justice William Rehnquist is given the same amount of time and inflection as a piece about the frog-jumping contest in Calaveras County and the latest advertisement for underarm deodorant. Often commercials are presented by people who have tangential relationships to news programs such as Willard Scott, Frank Blair and John Cameron Swazye. To the viewer this melange of news, entertainment, commercial information and personalities becomes an immense stew— confusing and unconnected to any relevant informational center of gravity.

You would think that television's experience with news and entertainment would be such that it would worry and perhaps warn other practitioners of journalism. Unfortunately, this does not seem to be the case. In fact, the printed press appears to be adopting a good deal of methodology that television has employed to make its news operations more profitable. The proliferation of consultants, food and living sections, and emphasis on graphics portends an ominous future. Recently, *Time* and *Newsweek* seemed to be in a desperate race to see how fast they could put Bruce Springsteen or Madonna on their covers. If television news has become entertainment, can printed news be far behind, and what will happen to the competition in print media if recent predictions that national advertising will decrease over the next few years as a consequence of more pinpointed and local marketing?

I agreed to share these observations in this space because Jack Hilton's advice and mine are essentially compatible for anyone who becomes immersed in this media configuration. Forthrightness and directness are sterling qualities much admired by Americans, who also can detect bombast and duplicity from great distances. They see and harshly judge when an interview subject is evasive or refuses to directly answer a question. As a journalist myself, I confess that my instinctive sympathies often lie with the dedicated reporter who seeks the truth. My contention is that when confronted by such a reporter who is trying to be fair and responsible, a person about to be queried by the press should not have any fears or misgivings. However, as a realist, I also know that some reporters are sometimes other than fair and responsible, either purposefully or stupidly. The key lesson from Jack is to *be prepared*—not necessarily for the worst, but *also* for the worst.

Hilton and I agree furthermore about the following point. In the overwhelming majority of contacts, meeting the press isn't warfare. To fear it is usually a perceptible signal to the viewer or the reader that you have something to hide.

So be prepared, say Hilton and I. Understand the environment and circumstances and all the rest. But play it straight. You and the American public will be the beneficiaries.

chapter one

How to
Meet the Press

This is a book about scoring points for yourself in press interviews on television (especially) and elsewhere (especially). That said, I now propose one quick diversion for purposes of context and perspective. (As they say in the broadcasting business: "We'll return to our main theme in just a moment.")

Years ago Senator Daniel Patrick Moynihan of New York made the following comment, which is still applicable. I don't think he intended it at the time, but he also defined the word *frustration* in a new way when he said:

> The American business system went on doing tolerably well, or better than that, but proved wholly incapable of making a case for itself [with the public]. It did justifiable things. It could not justify them. It did admirable things. It could not make them seem admirable.

If so, the blame for those failures must be laid at the doorstep of faulty public relations, often called PR (sometimes flippantly and disparagingly). PR also stands for press relations. The public gets most of its poop from the press, especially from the television medium.

A mentor of mine once said: "PR is a mirror." (Actually it's more than a mirror, but that's a fair start.) He said, "Companies should do good things, and be credited for them."

1

If Mr. Moynihan's statement was correct that justifiable, even admirable "things" can be done by an entity, but the press and public may conclude differently (and, as a result, wrongly), that mirror to which my elder referred is somehow smudged or fogged. The images are therefore distorted to the detriment of the enterprise in question.

The Senator also might have included another parenthetical truth that isn't widely metabolized, particularly in business circles: Appearances are reality for most Americans. What seems to be so is what is so—period. For an institution (or for that matter, an individual) to do "well" and prove "wholly incapable" of selling that proposition to the people at large is (in no particular order of priority) paradoxical, exasperating, and sometimes ruinous.

Consider the case of the Hypothetical Company. To fulfill its commitments under the terms of a Pentagon defense contract, Hypothetical's management decided that a certain executive with particular skills and experiences should be transferred from one of its plant cities to another, apparently a sensible and justifiable move. The executive and his family reluctantly agreed to the disruption and trauma of relocating in the middle of a school year, perhaps not entirely an altruistic or patriotic decision, but admirable nevertheless. It put the right man in the right spot for the right job, facilitating a hurry-up program for the U.S. Department of Defense.

For reasons too mundane to enumerate, the man and his wife were compelled to make this move a few weeks before their new house was ready for occupancy. (If you're a peripatetic type, you probably remember from personal experiences of a nomadic nature that inconveniences and glitches aren't unusual, but commonplace.) For an interim period, Hypothetical arranged for the family to stay in a nearby motel at the company's expense, which was also justifiable—a wholly legitimate cost of relocation, entirely absorbed in the company's overhead (a part of which is charged to government contracts, and all other contracts).

I forgot to mention that the executive's traveling party also included the family dog, Fursten. And because dogs and motels are largely incompatible, Fursten was stashed (not happily) in a local kennel for the duration of the wait, which was added to the list of incidental expenses, all comparatively minuscule.

Unfortunately for Hypothetical, only the last part of my little parable was subsequently heralded in the press. The government expressed dismay or outrage (it varied in numerous reports) on receiving a bill from the contractor for boarding a dog! The attendant headlines and TV news reports made w-r-o-n-g-d-o-i-n-g seem implicit, badly tarnishing the company's reputation.

They thought they had done the right things. The contract was urgent, so they rushed to fulfill it. But not unlike a host of industrial firms, particularly the militaristic ones, Hypothetical didn't know how to meet the press. Maybe they didn't care. (Later they changed their minds, although it remains to be seen if they change their ways.) To my recollection, no one from that company ever explained their circumstances in public. And if this case history sounds familiar, I'm guessing that I've told you more about it in the last four paragraphs than you gleaned at the time from stories in the papers and on television. (Incidentally, while we're spelling, a different way to spell Hypothetical is G–e–n–e–r–a–l D–y–n–a–m–i–c–s.)

This book doesn't presume that you don't know how to spell. It does presume that you have a case to make for the American people, something to explain or justify, whether you come from the business world or any other world.

I hope to explain how.

But first (as they also say in the broadcasting business) a final presumption on my part concerning paranoia, which is justifiable sometimes also. Even if you don't work for General Dynamics, it's likely that many of you are at least a tad paranoid about the press. The rest of you are merely apprehensive about contacts with reporters. (Does anything here ring true?) It's another of my aims to help you overcome these psychoses, some of which may have their roots in past experiences of a bad variety with news organizations. (In other words, I won't suggest that you're hallucinating. My bedside manner is terrific.)

But About My Pedigree...

Right here in the top of the first inning, let's dispense with who I am (now that we both know something about you). For almost 20 years I have functioned largely unobserved, but probably not unsuspected, behind several thousand national figures (political, business, and sundry) who have had (and continue to have) the following things in common: a need, a motivation, a reason, or an inexplicable desire to MEET THE PRESS. (Not everything in the life experience is wholly justifiable, nor is everything always rational.) My job has been to aid them in presenting their personal selves and their cases to the American people, inevitably through the press. (Wait a minute! Not all of them wanted to appear. Some were compelled.)

But if you don't recognize my name, please indulge another short story—the second of many to follow. It helps to explain why people like me are usually unobserved, but probably not unsuspected.

In the last presidential election campaign, I was engaged as a pundit by WCBS-TV in New York City to do political commentaries on some of their news programs, although broadcasting is only my avocation now. Mainly I'm what is called a *media consultant* (sometimes an *image maker*), and the TV station's news department wanted me to explain to their audiences how I thought the principal candidates were faring in the press, especially on television.

I remember a particular night during the early primaries. I decided to describe the hierarchical nature of a national campaign, and I referred at one point in my dissertation to "that subculture of consultants who lurk behind the candidates."

After I finished, the program's anchorman called me on it. He said, "You used the word *lurk* in conjunction with campaign packagers *lurking*. That connotes to me someone who is up to no good. Did you use that word deliberately? Or did you think of what it might mean?"

4

Now I fancy myself as something of a wordsmith. Next to pictures, words are my primary tools. The word *lurk*, for instance, has three accepted meanings. On that particular television program, as I was talking about men and women whose names you've mostly never heard, I intended the third definition.

But the anchorman also was correct. The first two definitions of *lurk* are "to lie in wait, as in ambush," and "to move furtively; to sneak, slink." My definition was the last one, which is "to exist unobserved or unsuspected."

As a media consultant, I go about my lurking and slinking by first explaining what the media are. I know that sounds ungrammatical, but bear with me. It takes more than one medium to make the media. And the media and the press (television, radio, newspapers and magazines, which will be our mutual purview for the next 20 chapters) are the same things, okay?

The second thing I do as a media consultant is to recommend a short bibliography of reading materials for the edification of my clients, underscoring my conviction that print is a better conveyance of information than prattle from me or anyone else. The fact that I previously wrote one of the books which I ardently recommend, *ON TELEVISION! A Survival Guide for Media Interviews,* is a sheer coincidence.

In it, in 1980, I stressed the fact that television skills are essential for persons like you, because TV is disproportionately important and powerful in mass communications. Most of us, according to innumerable polls, get most of our news and information from the TV medium.

After his eradication by Ronald Reagan on Election Day in 1984, Walter Mondale said at a press conference in St. Paul, Minnesota, "Modern politics requires a mastery of television. I've never really warmed up to television, and, in fairness to television, it's never really warmed up to me."

My job is to warm you up, which this book is intended to achieve, because modern anything seems to require a mastery of television. My clients have run the alphabetical gamut from academicians, ambassadors, and archaeologists to undersecretaries and vivi-sectionists, including titans and moguls from banking and commerce, one Cuban revolutionary, uncounted litigators, thoraxic surgeons, economists and nuclear physicists, theologians of numerous stripes (no partridges, no pear trees), legitimate do-gooders of all descriptions and, to complete this list (which I shouldn't have started in the first place), one anesthesiologist. (We both stayed awake during my sessions with her.)

Marshaling Support

I also was lurking unobserved and unsuspected in 1980, so I asked a better-known person, Robert MacNeil of *The MacNeil/Lehrer Newshour* on PBS, to write the foreword for my *ON TELEVISION* book. Even today his essay still pertains, as follows:

In 1968, after years of interviewing people on television myself, I learned what it was to be interviewed. It was quite a revelation.

I appeared on a truncated version of the radio/television talk-show circuit to promote a book about television I had just published, called *The People Machine*. It never occurred to me that someone as experienced as I was at asking questions on television would find it so hard to answer them. But I did.

It was very difficult to dredge up from all I knew just the right material to respond to a question; to be sensational enough to tickle someone's curiosity, yet not distort or overstate the case for effect.

Even more difficult for me was the required compression. I am a very wordy fellow once I get going, a natural essay-type answerer. My wife says that if you ask me a question, you are likely to get a speech or a lecture in reply. I am also sensitive to qualifiers. I hate saying: this is so and that is not so, because I can often see many reasons why each may be partly so. Television does not love qualification. It hates the subjunctive voice. It was hell trying to squeeze all my wonderful thoughts into tough 100-word bursts with no equivocation. I was just getting warmed up when I would see the host's eyes begin to glaze over.

Even more frustrating was the knowledge that there on the pages of my book, lying virginal in the lap of the host, was everything I wanted to say, the thoughts neatly phrased, the facts logically marshaled. I kept thinking: if only I could remember just how I said it in the book.

The questions themselves also threw me. They always seemed to come from a different part of the forest from where my thoughts were. Some were very ignorant questions and some well informed. Some were mildly malicious and testing; most were well intentioned, even generous. But something put me off balance almost every time. The most upsetting questions were the extremely simple ones, like this, for instance: "What is wrong with TV news?" If you have just spent a year researching and writing a book on that topic, you don't know quite where to begin. You are tempted to throw out a terse, witty put-down (the kind that comes to mind while going to sleep that night) or to deliver an encyclopedic monologue.

Finally, what I found very disconcerting was the indifference in the eyes of the interviewers. Most of them managed to be professionally curious—they looked curious—but when I looked into their eyes, they weren't there. They were distracted.

It was on the Mike Douglas show that I learned the secret truth; being interviewed is a lot easier than interviewing. If you know what you are talking about—and if it isn't something you have reason to be ashamed of—it is not a difficult experience. It's far easier, say, than standing up and making a speech.

Following instructions from the publisher's public relations people, I went early to Philadelphia where the Mike Douglas show was taped and met the producer. He was a pleasant, somewhat distracted man, who was clearly going to be able to carry on living without knowing what I had to say to the world. He exuded an air which suggested that if they didn't have boring guests like me cluttering things up, they would have a far better show, and his wife and children would love him more.

Anyway, he got interested enough to ask me: "What do you want him to ask you?"

"What do you mean?" I said.

"What questions do you want Mike to ask?"

"Well," I gulped, "anything at all. I don't care."

The producer sighed, as the proprietess in a house of prostitution might sigh when shy clients need to be pushed into saying what they really want. "You realize that he hasn't read the book."

Finally I began dictating questions to the producer. It went slowly because, very efficiently, he was writing them directly on big cue cards with a squeaky felt-tip pen.

The taping began. Mike Douglas turned out to be one of those charismatic show business fellows who enfold you in their charm and professionalism. He had a knack of looking at me with the greatest interest and absorption, until his eyes flicked over my shoulder to the cue card to read the next question. His eyes then clicked back to mine again as he carefully listened to the answer. He stayed awake, the audience applauded a few times, and two fellow guests, who had actually read my book, waxed enthusiastic about it. I had just begun to think that I would like to do this for a living when it was over.

I went away with one lesson firmly learned, and being interviewed on television has never bothered me since that day. The lesson is: Know what you want to say, and use whatever questions you are asked to say it—briefly, along the way, you can actually address the questions put to you or not, as you choose. You can flatter the host by saying things like "That's a really interesting question," or "Now, I think that's the nub of the whole thing." Just don't get so *fixated* by the questions you are asked that you forget to make your points, assuming you have some.

The other thing I gradually learned is that practice helps. Being interviewed once is terrible. The fifth time is a lot better.

There is a distinction to be made here, and Mr. MacNeil is about to make it. Appearing on television, indeed, meeting with any kind of press, isn't always (or even usually) tantamount to involvement on your part in a volcanic news event. Nor will you always face a pure journalist when you are displayed for an interview on TV and radio. The likes of Oprah Winfrey, Gary Collins, and Regis Philbin command more air time on a daily basis than Peter Jennings and Lesley Stahl. There is a difference between hard news where you and they mostly stick to the facts, and fluff. Fluff predominates on television. Interviews of the bonbon variety are more common than Oriana Fallaci stress tests, as MacNeil explains further.

Television has become the mass journalism of our day. Without doubt it will remain so, but its preeminence will probably grow. Its journalistic output is not, however, confined to programs that carry the label "news." Publishing topical information or opinion is journalism, and American television and radio stations do a lot of that under other headings. They may think of such programs as entertainment, or public service, or religious broadcasting, or consumer information, but in the broadest sense it is all journalism, and it is also subject to the same regulations as news programs, for example, the Fairness Doctrine or the equal-time provision. (In fact, news programs may be exempt from some regulations that govern the rest.) Such "entertainment" programs are also clearly governed by the laws against libel and slander. In other words, the stations are as responsible for the content of non-news shows as they are for the content of news programs. Yet very different standards apply.

The talk-show host like Mike Douglas is far more a law unto himself than the television newsman. He can be as eccentric as he likes in his choice of subjects. He can get by with no preparation and play it by ear, whatever the interview situation. He can argue with his guests, challenge their views, make jokes at their expense, air his own prejudices, and generally play God—no one will bat an eye. He is not even required to ask questions a journalist would consider relevant. He need never be burdened by mere facts. All he must follow is his own inner ear, his sense of what his audience will find interesting or amusing.

Such programs *may* be as responsible as TV news. Some may be a good deal more responsible, but often they are so freewheeling, so improvised, and even sometimes so irresponsible that it is not surprising for an inexperienced guest from the world of business or the professions to feel bewildered and defenseless. The frame of reference is vague; he doesn't know whether he is there to be laughed at, harangued, or applauded.

Here comes another good thought and admonishment from MacNeil about the second peril frequently inherent in TV and radio interviews: editing, which is sometimes known as emasculating. (The first peril is the interview itself.)

It is on the local television news that a person interviewed needs to be wary. Few news interviews are done "live." Most are recorded on film or tape, taken back to the studio, and a "bite" selected from all that was shot to represent the interviewee's side of the story. That bite may be as brief as fifteen seconds or as long as a few minutes, even though the camera crew and the reporter on the scene will have shot many times that amount. The bite that is selected may or may not represent the thrust of what the person interviewed intended to say. It may convey no glaring misrepresentation of his position yet leave a definite feeling that that wasn't how he intended to say it. It may have been a response drawn from him in answer to a question and yet presented in a way that suggests he volunteered the statement, a standard device of newspapers and wire services that makes people feel they have been quoted "out of context."

With television increasingly replacing newspapers as the source of competitive journalism in many cities, that cry is heard more often. Something about television makes the practice seem more egregious because, by its very nature, television is more credible. Surveys continue to show that more people get their news from television and find it more trustworthy than they do newspapers or magazines. Just to see and hear a man on television has some power to make you believe that what you see is what he said. Yet it may be only a small, and possibly prejudicial, part of what he said.

There are ways of coping with the danger: officers of corporations who are likely to be spokesmen on television when a news story breaks can school themselves in ways of keeping their message short and quotable as it stands. This book will help them do that. They can, if they wish, insist that their interview be run unedited. Many stations will balk, but some will go along.

Now a succinct description by MacNeil of the most commonplace problem in press relations (about which I intend to harp further—later). But in the following passage, press relations is a misnomer. Press unrelations is a better name for it, and therein lies the problem.

Learning all the tricks is not a substitute for having a good case, and it is fatal to leave good press relations until a crisis forces the issue. Businesses would be wise to practice what politicians have done for years. They cultivate and befriend TV newsmen when there is no crisis. It is not a question of "buying" the journalist, but educating him in the concerns and the realities of whatever the business is. When there is a crisis, or a hot news story, that newsman will at the very least be more receptive to your point of view. In fact, I don't share the widespread impression that television is out stalking business executives to make fools of them. Television newsmen line their studies with congratulatory plaques from business associations, not the scalps of company officers.

It is fashionable in television to apply the investigative label without much discrimination—it has a modish ring and makes a news show sound aggressive—but that shouldn't frighten anyone off. It is also the style of the moment to ask questions in a tough, belligerent manner to convey the impression that the newsman isn't letting the subject get away with anything. That fashion of interviewing was made irresistibly popular by *60 Minutes,* and its imitators will probably be with us for some years. But that is a matter of style, not substance.

While there are exceptions, I find the news media in this country rather deferential of the fact that the American psyche is rather hospitable to business. Nowhere is the making of things and their buying and selling considered a more worthy and respectable occupation of man's energies than in the United States. And the media reflect that underlying belief, even if they seem to growl at every businessman they see.

There certainly are exceptions, and I won't attempt to sell that "deferential" thesis to anyone at General Dynamics (which, incidentally, is *not* a client of mine).

Robert MacNeil's foreword in my previous book mainly focuses on *interviews* with reporters and program hosts in which the press obtains a goodly part of the news and information that it subsequently (or simultaneously) transmits to you. Interviews, America's oldest and most popular contact sport, are a prime focus of this book, too.

In terms of their impact on the public, the most important of these interviews are likely to occur on television. My phone at the office rang for a week after I was profiled a decade ago on the front page of *The Wall Street Journal*. It rang for three months after I appeared with Mike Wallace on *60 Minutes*. (Many of my callers and friends wanted to know what Mike is really like. Keep reading. I plan to tell you.)

Fairness, Equal Time, and Other Canards

MacNeil also mentioned the equal-time provision and the Fairness Doctrine in his dissertation, which many people get mixed up, so let me explain. You may never become embroiled with either statute but, if you're intending to play this game, it's helpful to know about the rules in force.

Section 315 of the FCC Code provides equal time for competing political candidates, except on news programs. (If that isn't you, don't go clamoring to a station demanding equal time to answer some nut.) It says in essence that TV and radio stations are obliged to make air time available to all declared candidates for a particular office, if any one of the candidates is given time. Please notice that I said all declared candidates, not just Democrats and Republicans, or all major candidates. (Who decides who's major and minor?)

In practice, that rule explains why political candidates in battles royal for elective office are seldom invited to appear on America's so-called talk show circuit. It isn't that prominent and charismatic politicos are disdained, but because a welcoming station would be eventually forced to accommodate all the other candidates, too, their obscurity notwithstanding.

Take for example the New Hampshire primary in February, 1984. A grand total of 22 Democrats answered the bell for that presidential race. If you were paying close attention at the time, maybe you can remember 8 of their names. (Maybe only 7, because one New Hampshire voter said he thought Reuben Askew was a sandwich!)

But in addition to Askew, Mondale, Alan Cranston, John Glenn, Gary Hart, Ernest Hollings, Jesse Jackson, and George McGovern, there were Martin Beckman ("Montana's Fighting Redhead"), Hugh Bagley (who wanted the U.S. to annex Mexico as our 51ST state), Gerald Willis (a wealthy timber baron), and 11 others whose names even I forget.

Among the contenders on the Republican side in New Hampshire were David Kelley (the last Confederate soldier) and the 76-year-old boy wonder of American politics, Harold Stassen.

At the time, I called the Federal Election Commission in Washington to get my facts straight and learned that a national total of 163 aspirants had filed applications for President Reagan's job, not an unusual number (believe it or not).

It would have made a whale of a talk show, no?

For the rest of us normal people, the Fairness Doctrine applies, a provision added by Congress in 1949 to the 1934 Communications Act. It says in summary that TV and radio audiences have the right to hear all sides of a controversial argument, if any one side is presented by a station. It works like this:

You're a member of the municipal beautification committee, let's say, and a staunch environmentalist. The preservation and up-keep of your town's remaining parks is your main objective. You are opposed in that view by a consortium of merchants, which proposes construction of a shopping center and access roads on the present site of Mulberry Gardens. Their representative appears on a local talk show to push his plan.

Maybe the mayor is an ally of yours, and you both appeal to the station manager for time to reply. Remember now, neither of you has a *right* to appear but, at least in the spirit of the Fairness Doctrine, the audience has a right to hear the opposing view(s). If yours and the mayor's opinions are similar, one of you will get on, and it will probably be you, because politicians are assumed to have ulterior motives. (There's always a looming election, isn't there?)

You may not appear on the same program where the merchant held forth; you will not necessarily be on at the same time of day or

13

the same day of the week. If your businessman opponent was interviewed for 10 minutes, maybe you'll be good for 15, or only 5. But somewhere, sometime on that station's schedule, the beautification committee will have its say in response.

Balance Doesn't Mean Equilibrium

In practice it's the imposition of those fairness principles that explain why station managers and other broadcasters in America are downright manic about balanced coverage of everything, including truly controversial or contested issues such as General Dynamics versus the Department of Defense. As a result, broadcasting is frequently the battleground for conflicts and confrontations. Name it. On virtually any matter, two (or more) combatants will likely be afforded air time to express their views, albeit an extremely short time, especially on newscasts (where these statutes don't apply per se, but are nevertheless commonly practiced in the interests of balance).

For instance, a 30-minute TV program like the *CBS Evening News* is really about 22 minutes of substantive content and 8 minutes of commercials, teasers, and other merriment. For purposes of this hypothetical model, let's say that a like number of 22 different stories and reports or mentions of newsworthy events are included on a typical broadcast, which sometimes happens. If the time were to be apportioned evenly among them (which it isn't), each story would be allocated about 60 seconds on the clock.

In every story the thesis is presented first, followed by evidence and examples. Let's say 20 seconds are gone already. Saving 10 seconds for a summary or conclusion leaves a final increment of 30 seconds for the protagonist and antagonist to be seen and heard, approximately 15 seconds each.

Adding a bit of perspective, 15 seconds of time at my rate of conversational speech equals about 43 words. (Adding further perspective, Walter Cronkite once said that all of the spoken words on a customary *Evening News* would fill less than three narrow columns on the front page of *The New York Times.*)

Even if the chairman of General Dynamics had called a press conference for TV crews and explained the circumstances of their dog boarding at length, perhaps only 15 seconds of his plea would have been excerpted and used by the networks and stations on their nightly newscasts, and these would probably be juxtaposed with 15 seconds of rebuttal or retribution by someone from DOD.

Had he tried it (and I am not aware that he did) his challenge would have been to relate and justify a rationale and course of action to dispassionate viewers in 43 words, which is the number of words included in this paragraph.

That isn't much, is it?

This constraint is not unknown to media consultants. If I had been hired to advise the aforementioned chairman, I might have worked to develop colorful, comprehensive and well-turned statements in 15-second bursts for him to utter at the conference, which doesn't ensure that any one of the bursts would have been excerpted intact by CBS and the other networks, but it greatly improves the chances.

In most TV interviews, as Robert MacNeil has noted, one key to success is brevity. (Making sensible points in a hurry and succinctly requires forethought and practice, another major thesis to be developed in subsequent chapters.) Even on the *Today Show* or *Good Morning America,* an interview segment with Jane Pauley or Joan Lunden isn't apt to be longer than 4 minutes. If the two of you share that time equally, which is not an uncommon occurrence when you're in the presence of a loquacious broadcaster, 2 minutes will be dominated by the interviewer, leaving you with approximately the same amount of time. Again, I'll use my rate of speech to illustrate, because it isn't exceptional. At about 172 words per minute (uninterrupted, which rarely happens on television or radio) 2 minutes may be 344 spoken words. If you are obliged in your early-morning interview to answer 8 questions in that allotted time before the intrusion of the next commercial, guess how many seconds are available on average or proportionately for each response? About 15, or approximately 43 words.

Of course, some interviews are longer, mostly those appearing on Sunday mornings, late at night, and on the radio, where audiences are also smaller. Some of them are live and others are taped to time, meaning they're prerecorded to the exact allotment of air time, and subsequently shown unedited. But the stations or programs decide about editing and excerpting. You don't. (I differ with Robert MacNeil when he says you "can insist" that an interview "run unedited. Many stations will balk, but some will go along." Despite the fact that my mother advised me never to use this word, that's never been my experience in 30 years of broadcasting, insisting notwithstanding.)

Magazine and newspaper reporters conduct interviews, too, many of them on the telephone. Essentially a press conference is a mass interview, with 20 or 200 questioners competing simultaneously for your attention. Managing those "events," and acquitting yourself smashingly, is what this book is all about.

A Final Word

Let us conclude this preamble with a comment of my own about Senator Moynihan's observation that business leaders and others don't make their cases very well with the public at large. Most people are lacking in sophistication and rudimentary knowledge when it comes to dealing with the media, which deliver their messages and convey their images.

In short, most people don't know HOW TO MEET THE PRESS.

chapter two

A Bouillabaisse

Okay, everybody out of the pool. It's time for the obligatory briefing about the press—its scope, location, nature, abundance, and other assorted data—over which I intend to skim as fast as possible because this book isn't a directory, friends.

My purpose here is twofold. There are literally thousands of places where you could be interviewed by the press, and you should know, at least generally, where they are. You also should know who you're talking to *primarily* (the reporter, or whatever you care to call the other person who participates in these dialogues) and *ultimately* (the audience, which is sometimes limited and sometimes vast). It's important for book readers to know this stuff. It says so in the writer's guide.

I call this chapter "A Bouillabaisse" because the collective press in America is, well, a bouillabaisse. (Bouillabaisse is a fancy name for stew with lots of weird ingredients.) Let's start with the pertinent statistics, although these numbers have a way of changing without notice, mostly owing to attrition and enterprise.

What the Reading Public
is Reading—and Where

At last count in the United States 1,688 newspapers were circulating their daily editions to 63,000,000 readers. On Sundays alone 783 papers are fingered by 57,000,000 people. At my house each paper is perused every day by at least two persons. At the office papers arriving in the possession of my fellow commuters are subject to further distribution, too, sometimes in the form of clippings or tear sheets.

Ditto for the magazines to which we subscribe at work (about 60 per month). Each magazine is routed to 10 or 15 staff members. (In the publishing trade this is known as pass-on readership, which accounts for a significant underground circulation.) Sixty may sound like a lot of magazines, but it's only .0054103 percent of the total number available to voracious readers according to the Magazine Publishers Association. They report that 11,090 different magazines are circulated in America, many of them relatively obscure and esoteric.

That raises a significant point; the distinction between a mass medium and the others. If mass for purposes of our deliberations is defined as the majority of the American people, most media of any description don't reach it. In the main (with the exception of *USA Today*) newspapers are local, and therefore limited geographically. If your pitch to preserve Mulberry Gardens is primarily intended for the denizens of South Bend, Indiana, the *San Diego Union* obviously won't tumble for the story. (Similarly, on local television in New York City no time was allocated for me to comment on the results of the Guam primary caucus in April of 1984, although the candidacies at stake were national and presidential. Nor, I suppose, was anyone in Guam particularly interested in New York's tenement fires and muggings on the same day.)

The wire services are the closest we come in the United States to mass print: Associated Press (AP), United Press International (UPI), and Reuters (which is not U.S. based). AP claims 7,200 subscribing organizations to which its news reports and other materials are fed: 1,500 newspapers and 5,700 television and radio stations. UPI is a distant second (and perpetually teetering on the brink of financial collapse) with 806 newspapers, 440 TV stations, and more than 1,000 radio stations. In total, Reuters has 150 U.S. subscribers, including the television and radio networks.

A *Bouillabaisse*

Bring the Urban Development Secretary to Mulberry Gardens for a major pronouncement about the preservation of city parks and an account of that oration will hum on the wire services to all subscribing news organizations, whereupon the recipients decide whether to run those hummings in their papers and on the air. (The options are local.)

By contrast, most magazines aren't confined geographically, but neither are they absorbed by the multitudes. They cultivate special audiences and constituencies, mainly appealing to comparatively spare numbers of people who are bonded by any commonality of interests or purposes.

In the days of yore, such magazines as *Liberty, Collier's, Life, Look* and *The Saturday Evening Post* were targeted for general circulation to the mass audience of Americans. But with the advent of network television, which displaced them for the majority, these magazines soon folded. TV sets now repose in almost 100 percent of U.S. households, and during the prime time evening hours 74 percent of those receivers in use, the critical mass, are tuned to one of the three commercial networks—ABC, CBS or NBC.

There's No Business Like Show Business

Local TV and radio outlets are also numerous. They are sufficient to accommodate any mope with a piece to speak. According to *Broadcasting* magazine 541 commercial TV stations are currently operating on the VHF band (channels 2 through 13 in any city). VHF stands for very high frequency. Higher than that is ultra high frequency (UHF)—north of channel 13—where 379 additional stations, all commercial, now reside.

We also have what some people call educational TV in America: 113 VHF stations and 186 Us, all of them aligned with the Public Broadcasting Service (PBS).

Of the commercial stations, 637 are affiliated with ABC, CBS, or NBC, meaning they have ironclad agreements to run some or all of the national programming in their local communities. More than 250 other TV outlets are affiliated with none of the networks; these are the so-called independent television stations.

Really, though, most stations are independent—and all of them are locally licensed by the Federal Communications Commission (FCC)—because the vast majority of the TV stations, although affiliated, are not owned by the networks. In fact, the networks own only four or five stations apiece.

ABC

WABC-TV, New York
KABC-TV, Los Angeles
WLS-TV, Chicago
WXYZ-TV, Detroit
KGO-TV, San Francisco

CBS

WCBS-TV, New York
KCBS-TV, Los Angeles
WBBM-TV, Chicago
WCAU-TV, Philadelphia

NBC

WNBC-TV, New York
KNBC-TV, Los Angeles
WMAQ-TV, Chicago
WRC-TV, Washington
WKYC-TV, Cleveland

Breaking the monotony of this boring data is the following explanation of call letters such as WXYZ and KGO. In the dim, distant past it was decided by the FCC (virtually everything in broadcasting is initials and acronyms) that stations situated east of the Mississippi River would be designated by a "W" prefix, stations west by a "K." Of course, there are exceptions to every rule, further complicating this dissertation. Before that FCC decree, a few stations already existed (for example, KDKA in Pittsburgh). They were permitted to keep their original Ks or Ws under terms of a grandfather clause (GFC).

Back to the bouillabaisse. Lately in America we have witnessed the advent of cable TV; the nation is approximately 45 percent wired. At present 6,553 cable systems are operational, serving almost 33,000,000 subscribers.

Radio is even more abundant than television. Nine thousand eight hundred and forty-nine stations are currently licensed: 4,799 AM, 3,839 FM, 1,211 educational FM.

Not including the cable TV systems (few of which originate programming as opposed to merely transmitting it), there are 11,068 broadcasting outlets in the United States, a tremendous proliferation in recent decades. On the schedules of virtually all of them are regular programs (daily, weekly, or at least monthly) where the likes of you might be given a shot.

Eleven thousand transmitters going full-blast! That's what's called a cacophony, and you might as well join in. I suggested several pages ago that you may never become embroiled with either the Fairness Doctrine or section 315 of the FCC Code. That's because most people aren't accepted for interviews on television and radio as a result of brute force. Usually they're invited to appear—a voluntary act—even welcomed. These welcomes at thousands of broadcasting stations occur every hour on the hour. In between hours, too. (This presumes that the aforementioned guests have something to say, about which an audience may give a damn.)

You as a fascinating conversationalist, you in your representative capacity, are grist for a broadcaster's mill. And mostly you come for free, because hardly any interviewees or newsmakers are paid for the privilege. Several minutes of air time are burned off, the audience is sufficiently engrossed to stay tuned, Mulberry

Gardens is saved, the station sells a couple of advertisements for cash money, and everyone lives happily ever after (except, perhaps, the merchants' consortium).

Another *"Final Word"*

Before this briefing ends, it should be forcibly established and stressed that commercial broadcasting in America is wholly a business, not a religion. (On second thought, even a religion is at least partly a business.) Most publishing is likewise. Provocative headlines about boarding a German shepherd at the government's expense, sometimes printed in red ink by tabloids such as Rupert Murdoch's, *sell newspapers,* which increases circulation thereby enticing more advertisers.

On TV and radio the equivalents of circulation are audience shares and ratings. The higher they both are, the more revenue is realized and deposited from the sale of each commercial announcement, which is how the proprietors keep score.

The top brass in broadcasting are *salesmen,* mostly. Things like truth and objectivity are deemed important in what Edwin Newman correctly calls "the news business," but everything else is subordinated to profit. Broadcasting revenue accumulates by attracting the rapt attention of masses of people whose residences are within range of a station's antennae—period. It therefore follows that *mass communications,* by the very definitions of those words, cannot be *esoteric.*

I also said in the first chapter that the most important and credible of your interviews with the press are likely to occur on commercial television, where the audiences are largest and the reach is extensive. Most American households have at least one TV set, and the occupants of those dwellings stare at it for an average of 7 hours and 10 minutes per day, approximately 2,600 hours per year, which is more than they do anything else, including sleeping and working.

A Bouillabaisse

The gifted and brilliant communications theorist from the University of Toronto, the late Marshall McLuhan, once referred to us as a "visually-biased society." He and Robert MacNeil (among others) have observed that seeing is believing. Eighty-three percent of what we learn comes from what we see. (Eleven percent from what we hear.) Fifty percent of what we remember is both seen and heard, which is television's forte.

So let us hold newspaper reporters and the others in abeyance until later chapters and turn our primary attention to the television interview, which our forefathers didn't envision. In the late-18TH century the press in America was wholly print, which accounts for Thomas Jefferson's choice of words in 1787 when he wrote the following in a letter to Colonel Edward Carrington: "Were it left to me to decide whether we should have a government without newspapers, or newspapers without a government, I should not hesitate a moment to prefer the latter."

He later changed his mind.

Jefferson and the other Founders had contemplated the press as an institution that would challenge authority and the status quo, be undisciplined, and even be somewhat irresponsible.

They probably didn't contemplate those challenges to the authority and status of their successors in the form of interrogations at press conferences and on news programs by impeccably groomed, magnificently tailored, and marvelously powdered television stars. They didn't foresee annual stipends for news personalities in roughly the range that might be paid in ransom to free the first-born son of Prince Charles. And surely they harbored no expectation that TV newscasters would have their appearance contracts negotiated by theatrical agents.

Dan Rather is grossing $25 million for these ten years under his current agreement at CBS News. NBC's Tom Brokaw isn't far behind. Even at the local stations in major cities, news broadcasters command $500,000 per year—and many of them are airheads. Let's cut them some slack, however. It is patently true that Ted Baxter on the nightly news isn't a Rhodes scholar. But neither is Ted's program a scholastic

23

aptitude test. Anchormen and women are paid astronomical sums because they appeal to their audiences, and (a related point) because the networks and stations for which they toil are profitable on the verge of unconscionable or euphoric.

Salaries in TV journalism are a persistent irritant to newspaper reporters who are paid comparative pittances. One of the latter, employed by a publisher in Brooklyn, once wrote: "It is difficult to believe, but television reporters are getting paid well into six figures to stand in front of a burning building and tell us it's on fire."

Even at those levels of compensation, we're now talking about the galley slaves of the television business. That same reporter on the scene who also interviews the Fire Marshal may have three other stories to cover, including yours, before rushing back to the studio to edit the tapes in time for the evening newscast. In those circumstances, most of the cerebral activity in which a reporter may engage is taking place during the interview itself. He or she has arrived perhaps 10 minutes beforehand, with just enough time to sketch in the barest details of the fire before the questioning begins on camera. Although these people may sound more relaxed than their subjects, the demands of their jobs provide for little more than a once-over of the physical facts of a story.

Knowing Your Stuff

Faced with the likes of you as a knowledgeable interviewee, such a reporter can only defer to the person with greater expertise about the subject at hand. And unless you happen to be talking about a topic that was the reporter's minor in college, the chances of your being outclassed or embarrassed by the fine points of an interviewer's sophisticated questions are slim indeed.

Objection to my derogatory comment will be registered by at least some of the above-mentioned airheads, so I'll step aside for one paragraph of supporting testimony. Charles Kuralt, who works "On the Road" for the *CBS Evening News*, has probably seen more boondock television than anybody else alive, one motel at a time. "My overwhelming impression of all those hours in all those years is of *hair,*" he once reported. "Anchormen's hair. Hair carefully styled and sprayed, hair neatly parted, hair abundant, and every hair in place. There's a big improvement in hair styles, but I can't remember much that came out from beneath all that hair. And I fear that the reason may be there wasn't much substance there. I am ashamed—I think we all ought to be ashamed that 25 years into the television age, so many of our anchormen haven't any basis on which to make a news judgment, can't edit, can't write, and can't cover a story."

It may be hard to understand why stations are so concerned with appearances, frequently at the expense of meaningful communication and intelligent discourse. Perhaps it helps to be reminded once again that television stations are not run by people whose primary mission is improving the flow of information. Remember, the stations are businesses; there is no compelling reason to change unless the pelf stops rolling in, which is a fact the occasional crusader for better TV news usually learns the hard way.

It is important to keep this profile of local stations in mind because, at least to begin with, that's where you'll be appearing. Like the newspaper business, television and radio are local media, too—overwhelmingly so. However, unless you happen to be a Fire Marshal or a Mafia don, it isn't likely that most of your local interviews will take place in the streets. You won't always and only be questioned by broadcast journalists in the strictest sense, because Phil Donahue and the legion of his clones in America don't report to anybody's news department. Most frequently, television interviews are conducted (1) in studios, and (2) on so-called talk shows where hosts and hostesses can be seen at virtually any hour of the day and night, lounging around on overstuffed furniture, engaging in red hot or banal conversations with government figures, rock singers, indicted felons, soap opera stars, authors, broken-down movie actresses, world travelers, fashion designers, boutique owners, cosmeticians, overly plump home economists, sex experts, and motley others. Fitting you in to such a program lineup should be no problem if what you stand for, stand accused of, or propose is sufficiently arresting or controversial.

If you think there's a certain "Gong Show" mentality in broadcasting (a tendency on television and radio to give precedence to the flamboyant personality or the oddball idea as opposed to mainstream opinion) you may proceed to the head of the class. (It's doubtful that's exactly what Mr. Jefferson and his peers had in mind when they encouraged the press to be unruly and irascible.) What's the point of having someone on the air to defend nutrition? If everyone agrees that red lights mean stop, there is no point in inviting an advocate of stopping at red lights to appear on a talk show. If you can find an advocate of fuchsia lights, assuming there is some reasonable explanation for this passion, that's news. News talks about change, about the things that upset the status quo. The more people you want to rattle by your proposal, the more likely it is that you will get air time to speak your piece. And if your idea is quirky, like the tongue-in-cheek campaign to put underwear on naked farm animals, they'll be clamoring for you to appear.

There you will sit in one of the aforesaid television studios, confronted by a local interviewer who, as Robert MacNeil has said, is mostly unconstrained and largely ungoverned.

chapter three
A Baker's Half-Dozen

This isn't scientific, but a discerning observer can identify at least six different interview types on television and radio, some of which occasionally overlap.

First is the *inquisition*. Mike Wallace all but invented it 30 years ago in New York City on a dimly lit local show called *Night Beat*. (Primarily what got "beat" were the nightly participants who volunteered to appear so Mike could be strict with them. "None of my guests is suicidal," said Wallace at the time. I remain unconvinced.)

So-called inquisitorial interviews are where the guests start off guilty and remain guilty until proven innocent, which rarely happened on *Night Beat*.

Here's an example from my own experience.

Twenty years ago in Chicago a client of mine, a senior executive from the Ford Motor Company, was invited to appear on television to explain a factory recall of certain cars. The man was nearing his 65TH birthday and mandatory retirement after more than 40 years in the service of that company. In fact he had been hired before the Great Depression by Henry Ford himself. The founder was his benefactor, and the two men became fast friends.

For the television program in Chicago, the Ford executive had been prepped exhaustively about the defect that prompted the mass recall and was armed with statistics and other goodies. But, unbeknownst to my client, the program host had additional plans for the interview. Certainly the recall would be covered in the quarter-hour segment, but the host also was interested in the legendary Mr. Ford, who passed away in 1948. He hadn't interviewed anyone else who actually knew the founder of Ford.

In his reading beforehand, the host learned that Mr. Ford also was engaged for a time in another business in the 1920s as owner and publisher of *The Dearborn Independent*, a teeny newspaper in the Detroit area. Mr. Ford wrote occasional essays for the paper, several of which were duly collected by the host, who concluded as a result that the auto magnate was blatantly anti-Semitic.

That would be a nifty tack for the interview: anti-Semitism in America during the Industrial Age. (Incidentally, the host's name was David Baum—decidedly a pro-Semitic person.)

On the program, dispensing with the recall in two minutes flat, Mr. Baum asked the Ford executive for reminiscences about his former boss, and the car man gladly obliged. Better (my client reasoned) to use the remaining TV time discussing a glorious heritage than dwelling on defects and other malfunctions.

Baum wanted to know about Mr. Ford, the man, and his outside interests. He cited a few lines from one of Henry Ford's columns in the *Independent*, a number of which were stacked on his lap.

"Did it ever trouble you," Baum inquired, "to be employed by, and associated with, an apparent anti-Semite?"

The Ford executive (suddenly less enthusiastic) murmured something about bygones being bygone. "That was a long time ago," he said.

Baum cited another statement from an old column, the second more inflammatory than the first, then a third, then a fourth (the last ones in rapid succession).

It was razzle-dazzle television—in the host's view.

"Forget employment," said Baum stridently. (Temperatures were rising.) "How in good conscience could a seemingly decent man like you look in the mirror each morning, knowing you were beholden to a bigot like Henry Ford?"

By now the car man's exasperation and embarrassment were extreme. Red-faced, stuttering at first, he finally exclaimed: "Dammit, Dave! There's a bad apple in every barrel!"

Fortunately for Ford (and my friend), that exchange was never seen on Chicago television. It took place in a private workshop that I ran, although it seemed real at the time to my visitor from Detroit. The studio and cameras were real. The crew was real. The lights were blazing. Every aspect of the TV experience was carefully staged and simulated.

I did it to teach several lessons, all of which are applicable today.

Lesson #1: All of us occasionally say things extemporaneously that we don't really mean.

Lesson #2: Never underestimate your opposite number in an interview. Some of them do their homework.

Lesson #3: Avoid inquisitorial interviews unless subpoenaed.

Next on our list is *hard news,* which is frequently gleaned at the scene of a catastrophe (we're back on the street, neighbors, but only for a moment), and these interviews are easiest for the novice to follow because reporters are taught from cubbyhood to base them on the H and the five Ws: "Tell us, Miss LaRue, *who* was the victim? *What* was he doing in the massage parlor with the industrialist when the fire broke out? *Where* were you? *When* did you start working for Friendly Fingers? *Why* do you think the tycoon ran back into the burning building when the police and fire trucks arrived? *How* did the fire start?"

It's not fancy; it's not inventive. But it works.

Some of television's less penetrating reporters have added another stock question, and it has become so common that it almost rates a listing of its own in third place as an interview type. It's called *how do you feel?* (Reporters sound like amateur psychologists when they ask it.) It goes like this:

A prominent civic leader has just pleaded nolo contendere to a swindling charge. Sentencing is scheduled in 10 days. His name is emblazoned in headlines on the front pages of the morning tabloids. His friends have deserted him; his reputation has plummeted to near zero. On the steps of the courthouse, a rookie reporter from the local television station rushes up and asks how he feels. Taped footage is later shot of the reporter nodding grimly and severely. On that night's newscast, the nodding footage is intercut with the condemned man's pitiful answer.

First cousin to hard news is the *in-depth* interview, which is also called *informational.* These discourses aren't limited to the whos, whats, and whens of a topic. They're intended to probe deeper, to reveal more. They elicit just plain interesting things from a respondent (especially secret and confidential things), which doesn't necessarily ensure the purity or honesty of what is revealed. (Over the years a silo-full of unadulterated bullshine has been conveyed to well-intentioned reporters during informational interviews.)

It isn't predominantly the goal of in-depth interviewers to keelhaul their subjects (as the inquisitors do), but these encounters can nevertheless be stressful. It's said in retrospect that many a national figure gladly would have opted for a proctological exam over an interview on television by Lawrence Spivak on the original *Meet the Press.* (Ditto more recently for Sam Donaldson's targets on *This Week with David Brinkley*).

Next is the *entertaining* interview, for which Johnny Carson gets first prize. Johnny's interviews are more fun than foreplay with Bo Derek. But as the writer, Roger Kahn, once said, they're about as spontaneous as arson. The interviews are cooked up in advance by *Tonight Show* production assistants who commute beforehand between Johnny and his invited guests, tapping the latter for funny stories, and reporting the results to Carson. Writers thereupon concoct Johnny's ad-libs. Also, questions are written for Carson to garner the expected replies and anecdotes, which in turn trigger Johnny's carefully planned one-liners.

It's all choreographed like a classic ballet, and Johnny pulls it off masterfully night after night.

I'm having trouble with a name for the sixth type of interview, because it encompasses two different, but probably related, phenomena. It's the one where the reporter or program host (1) hasn't done any homework and/or (2) doesn't listen to the answers, which may signal that you are in the presence of a *nitwit*.

Robert MacNeil made reference in the first chapter to his newly-written book "lying virginal" on Mike Douglas's lap. It is not unprecedented or atypical. Stacked on other laps, in a similar condition, are printed materials of every kind (annual reports, environmental impact statements, your company biography, research studies), but authors are the quickest to take offense.

William F. Buckley, Jr. tells of an experience comparable to MacNeil's on another network television program.

"The entire hour would be given to my book," he once related. "I was brought in beforehand to visit briefly with the host in his makeup room. He reached out and shook my hand, then warmed me with the following words. 'Just got back from a week's vacation in Nassau. Took your book with me, but couldn't get past the first six pages.' I was affronted—but only for a very little while. After the first six minutes on the air with him, it became clear to me that he had never gotten past the first six pages of *any book*."

MacNeil also referred to that telltale "glaze" in his interviewer's eyes, frequently a tip-off that the man or woman isn't listening, but merely hopes to retain employment after four minutes on television or radio with a dullard like you. (Reporters who always ask how everyone feels are among the worst in listening to the answers—never mind the nodding.)

Let me show you how it works, because if you watch television long enough, you're sure to see this scenario played out someday:

SCIENTIST: "...and guess what we discovered in our laboratory which will save mankind?"

HOST: "Do you help your wife with the dishes?"

Lately the *ambush* interview also has emerged as a staple. Its principal exponent and practitioner was Geraldo Rivera, now but a memory at *ABC News*.

It's an ambush when a TV reporter and camera crew step abruptly and unexpectedly into your path from a darkened alley or

31

doorway. You, in turn, look like a startled coyote on the five o'clock news, or like a deer in headlights.

Dan Rather once exposed a crook on *60 Minutes* during an ambush interview in a meat locker.

Mike Wallace tried a few of them, too, but CBS subsequently decided that it wasn't dignified for a 70-year-old man to be leaping from the shrubbery.

If you remember MacNeil's Rule (to be reiterated on the next page) it's of little matter which type of interview may be upcoming for you. Preparation for any of them encompasses strategy and tactics.

For our purposes, strategy is the *substance* of what you intend to say or disclose. (Later we'll deal with tactics—your *performance*, in other words.)

chapter four
Be Prepared!

It is un-American to plagiarize the Boy Scouts, but I need to borrow their motto for purposes of this chapter.

At the outset, Robert MacNeil advised the following about press and television interviews: "Know what you want to say, and use whatever questions you are asked to say it." He also added, "Along the way, you can actually address the questions put to you or not, as you choose. Just don't get so *fixated* by the questions you are asked that you forget to make your points, assuming you have some."

Superior advice! I hesitate to suggest that you deface this handsome and expensive book, but if you remove this page and tape it to your bathroom mirror, you will be vastly improved as an interviewee.

Recently I was asked to submit an article about interview preparation to the editors of a monthly magazine for college presidents, and I said in my essay, "Maybe your football coach can be of service. The preparations correlate."

First comes a defensive game plan. Anticipate the questions that you may be asked. Decide beforehand how you'll answer. Ad-libbing in public on matters of importance is a no-no, but don't use a script either. Just get your salient points on each topic lined up in order of their importance and rehearse out loud.

Next comes offense. Novices are inclined to neglect it because they become obsessed with responding. But that's only part of a dialogue. The other part is stimulus. Ask yourself, "What in the world compelled me in the first place to accept this invitation to boil slowly under TV's hot lights? What do I want to accomplish for alma mater?" Don't be greedy, but you're certainly entitled to ventilate a few items of your own, not necessarily in response to someone else's questions. Remember, this is a *conversation,* not the Spanish Inquisition. Be prepared to take the initiative when the opportunities arise.

Once the game commences time of possession is important, too. Getting from defense to offense requires an exchange: a kick-off, punt, fumble, interception, or (I hope for you) a touchdown! In conversational dynamics an exchange occurs when one participant *bridges* another and seizes the initiative. A bridge gets you from where you are in a discussion to where you want to be, which is presumably on the safer ground of topics or points of your choosing (based on your previous decisions concerning the offensive game plan). Bridge is a term that I started using in 1970, and now it's commonplace in the lexicon. (Unfortunately, English words are impossible to copyright.) However, a bridge that doesn't fit because it's evasive or contrived, and so jars the audience, is called a bridge too far.

Successful bridging requires a smooth connecting phrase, clause, or sentence as a preface. "Let me put that matter in a slightly different perspective," or, "let's consider the larger issue here." (The permutations are endless.) If you're asked about a problem at your school, don't dwell on it unless it's the problem that you're aiming to discuss. Talk about the *solution*. If the past tense of an issue is awkward for you, bridge to the present tense or the future tense. Getting from the former to the latter is up to you; six or eight words of bridging should be sufficient to do the job.

Just remember two things MacNeil and I have been saying here.

1) Don't be fixated by the question(s); don't be confined or impaled by the specific or limited thrust of your interrogator's query;

2) and be alert for chances to go on offense, to take the initiative.

Be Prepared!

The advice pertains to college presidents and everyone else—notably you. It's easily said and done—if you persist.

In the last 15 or 20 years I have made hundreds of speeches on approximately this topic, mostly to men and women who are apprehensive about reporters: once burned, twice cautious. That accounts for why I have visited most of America's fabulous spas from coast to coast, which is where these groups are inclined to congregate. Not long ago I addressed several hundred members of the U.S. Congress at the Greenbrier Hotel in West Virginia, under the auspices of the Democratic Congressional Campaign Committee. (The night before, at a lavish banquet in the resort's main ballroom, we sat around the food-laden tables discussing hunger in America.)

In every one of these lectures, although I get to the point by circuitous (sometimes tortuous) routes, I have talked about an interviewee's attitude in anticipation of a press encounter. Attitude is fundamental and is usually a rookie's first mistake, thereby guaranteeing failure, or less than a socko performance, in an interview.

Just for a moment, but right now, put yourself in a newsmaker's place. This Sunday you will appear on NBC-TV's *Meet the Press*. After the hyperventilation subsides, what is your first semiconscious thought or consideration? "What questions will I be asked?" And, "How will I answer?" Be honest. That's what you're thinking, isn't it? If so (not that those questions are irrelevant) you are on a loser's track. You are preparing yourself (with sizable doses of trepidation) solely to respond, which immediately puts you in a reactive, or passive, mode. (In other words, you're probably doomed on Sunday, and *NBC* doesn't supply cigarettes or blindfolds.)

That's because your attitude and state of mind are ass backwards. One hundred fifty nine pages after the word respond appears in my dictionary, the word *stimulus* is listed, too, and is defined as "anything causing or regarded as causing a response. An agent, action or condition that elicits or accelerates a physiological or psychological activity. Something that incites or rouses to action." To *stimulate* is "to act or serve as a stimulant or stimulus."

It's an active, not reactive, role.

In essence I said in my article for the college presidents that *Meet the Press* isn't the Spanish Inquisition; it's a conversation that happens to occur on network television. Approach it in that sense attitudinally, and you immediately become a participant (not a respondent; not a pincushion).

Also remember that as a conversational *participant*, on television or anywhere else in the presence of reporters, you are still covered by the First Amendment to the U.S. Constitution. Neither Congress nor NBC shall make a law "prohibiting the free exercise... or abridging the freedom of speech...."

Are you getting the message?

If so you are finally in an acceptable state to commence the necessary preparations for Sunday. (If not please go back and memorize the last seven paragraphs.)

I'll bet I know what you're thinking as you evaluate all this palaver about offensive and defensive game plans, and especially pertaining to my assertion that ad-libbing in public on matters of importance is a no-no. You're thinking it's all terribly manipulative and contrived, aren't you? If I'm right you're permitted a second trip to the head of the class, because an accomplished newsmaker or national figure wouldn't meet the press any other way. There is no earthly reason why the word *contrive* should have a wholly negative connotation, just because its second definition is "to plot with evil intent." Its first definition is "to plan or devise with cleverness or ingenuity," and that's us at this moment as we get you ready for Sunday's *Meet the Press*.

So first let's dispense with ad-libbing, except, perhaps, for "thank you, Marvin" when Mr. Kalb introduces you on next week's program.

I remember holding a speech practice session several years ago with a national political candidate. He was trying out some new concepts and remarks on an issue raised only the day before by his opponent. The two of us were alone in a hotel room. At one point he paused midsentence for a few seconds. "I'm hearing *myself* for the first time," he said, "so please forgive me if I say something dumb!"

Better to say it in private than in front of 10,000,000 television viewers, agreed?

Only a consultant with an IQ lower than room temperature would permit you (or a candidate for political office) to ad-lib in front of an important audience, particularly a TV audience. The stakes are entirely too high; there is no chance for retraction or mollification, and history is replete with examples of the f–a–t–a–l g–a–f–f–e.

"There's a bad apple in every barrel," said my friend from Ford (perhaps truthfully, but certainly injudiciously). Luckily for him, he said it in a practice session (a private affair, and I happen to be the soul of discretion). Later he offered me $100,000 for the only copy of that videotape, and I don't think he was altogether kidding. Stupidly, I forked it over for free, which partly accounts for my current laboring with this text in a valiant attempt to provide more generously for my heirs.

George Romney (the former Governor of Michigan and, in 1968, a contender for the GOP nomination for president of the United States) wasn't as lucky. Asked one night on the radio in Detroit why he changed his stance on the Vietnam War, Mr. Romney ad-libbed, "I was brainwashed!" His candidacy was ended in terms of serious consideration by the American people before the next commercial could be cued. (Commenting on Romney's ad-lib the following day, Senator Eugene McCarthy from Minnesota wisecracked, "George Romney was brainwashed? A *light rinse* would have been sufficient.")

Of similar proportions was President Gerald Ford's gaffe in 1976, when he ad-libbed in the second TV debate with Jimmy Carter that Poland and Eastern Europe weren't dominated by the Soviet Union. Compounding it, Mr. Ford stuck to that story for several days afterwards (until he finally relented), making people wonder if the President of the United States had (1) bumped his head too hard or (2) read any newspapers since 1945.

In November Gerald Ford was retired to Aspen, Palm Springs, or Cucamonga (I forget which).

Not unlike preparing you for *Meet the Press*, the planning and forethought for presidential debates on television are exhaustive, too. In 1980, as Governor Reagan's advisers had anticipated, President Carter said in Cleveland's TV debate that Reagan had begun "his political career campaigning around this nation against Medicare." Carter concluded: "Governor Reagan, typically, is against such a proposal."

Failing to refute that allegation would have seriously damaged the Republican cause with millions of senior citizens and others. But refuting it too stridently would have risked offending more of us who prefer that our presidents be accorded respect, even deference.

How to express exasperation over an erroneous charge often repeated by Mr. Carter and, at the same time, a measure of respect for the president's office was the problem at hand for Ronald Reagan, and it finally was decided that the candidate would say: "There you go again!"

That statement was contrived by the Reagan advisers three days before the main event. And at the appropriate moment on stage at the Convention Center Music Hall in Cleveland, Candidate Reagan said, respectfully, "There you go again!" (LONG PAUSE.) "When I opposed Medicare, there was another piece of legislation meeting the same problem before Congress. I happened to favor the other piece of legislation, and felt it would be better for the senior citizens, and provide better care than the one that was finally passed. I was not opposing the *principle* of providing care for them. I was opposing one piece of legislation as versus another."

Crisis averted—in 71 words (approximately 25 seconds at my rate of speech, not counting the LONG PAUSE) and highly excerptable intact for the later TV newscasts.

In Mr. Reagan's view President Carter had misstated and misrepresented his position on medical care for the elderly and others. So the record was set straight on television with a seemingly spontaneous and unrehearsed exclamation by the former Governor (that was approximately as spontaneous and unrehearsed as a performance by the Joffrey Ballet).

Be Prepared!

To be truly *extemporaneous* is to have "spoken or otherwise performed with little or no preparation or practice," which no politician in his right mind is likely to do on *Meet the Press* or anywhere else in meeting the press. Extemporaneous speech combines these processes, composition and presentation, simultaneously. Because that's fraught with peril for a speaker much of my work as a consultant is aimed (yes, manipulatively, but not sinisterly) at separating the two.

This kind of forethought and preparation was demonstrated subsequently in the second TV debate in 1984 between President Reagan and Walter Mondale. After the President's frankly doddering performance in the first debate two weeks previously, senility became an issue in the campaign, and the Reagan brain trust anticipated a question from someone on the panel of reporters about the President's age.

On stage in Kansas City, they were accommodated in spades before 80,000,000 television viewers by Henry Trewhitt of *The Baltimore Sun*. And Mr. Reagan ad-libbed his reply just as he had written it on a legal pad several days before, flawlessly and verbatim: "I will not make age an issue in this campaign," he said. "I'm not going to exploit for political purposes my opponent's youth and inexperience."

Twenty three words, or about eight seconds at my rate of speech (not including the audience's explosive response). I'll wager $50 that you saw it on the late-evening newscasts of October 21ST, unless you were visiting the Australian outback. An additional $25 says that you'll see it replayed on television every four years until the tape wears out.

To anticipate an interviewer's questions beforehand doesn't necessitate an advanced degree in prescience. Even if you're not a swami or fortune teller, you can pull if off with remarkable competence provided you're an avid and conscientious reader. That isn't suggesting you should subscribe to 1,688 newspapers and 11,090 magazines. About six of the above will do it, as supplements to your local papers, as follows:*The New York Times*, *The Washington Post*,

The Wall Street Journal, The Los Angeles Times, Time, and *Newsweek,* the creme de la creme of American journalism.

If accounts of your issue or topic aren't reported on their pages you can be fairly sure that (1) nothing is happening or (2) no one cares. In either case, it merely means that you'll have less to anticipate from reporters, because they won't know what's going on either! (However, it also may mean that short of holding the aforementioned reporters at gunpoint it may be a problem getting anyone to talk to you.)

Reporters and television personalities are paid (the latter better than the former) to find out about topical, newsworthy, relevant, and interesting things (also momentous and weird things). If your crusade is none of the above, and can't be made to seem enticing, you are reading the wrong book.

But rather than stop writing in the middle of the fourth chapter, let us assume that you and your cause are newsworthy, which means two more things are likely.

1. The papers and magazines listed above are on the case,
2. and *all* other reporters and broadcasters (with precious few exceptions) have gleaned the totality of their information from the above-mentioned accounts. (That especially applies to the occupants of local TV and radio newsrooms, most of whom don't have a clue about what's happening when the papers and wire services aren't functioning.)

So if you can parallel an interviewer's preparation, you also can duplicate it; unless you recently came through a lobotomy, the same challenging questions will occur to you and everyone else.

It isn't likely that you'll phrase them the same, but if you do this exercise diligently you'll pinpoint the central thrust of every probable question in advance. And even if the convoluted or unique phraseology of a question surprises you when the interview takes place, remember MacNeil's advice: don't be fixated or mesmerized.

Now, presumably, you have written down the 25 likeliest questions which you can expect on *Meet the Press,* and let's say it's only Friday. Your date to appear before NBC's firing squad isn't until Sunday! Forty-eight hours to think up some boffo answers!

Let me interrupt this exercise to mention two provisos, please. In the first place, there won't be time on Sunday's program for anyone to ask 25 questions, unless you're planning to plead the Fifth Amendment in response to everything, so already you are over-prepared. (Feeling better? Comfort is proportionate to confidence. And confidence, in turn, is the result of forethought and deliberation: Be prepared!) Like any other client of mine, my hope and goal for you on Sunday's program is *no surprises* (most of which have a tendency to be unpleasant). But secondly, don't stop reading the papers on Friday, because the big ones (at least) also are published on Saturday and Sunday mornings. Some sneaky person at NBC is apt to be reading them and hoping against hope for a latest development or turn of events. You do likewise, please; preparation ends as performance begins—as you utter your first words on the air to a vast and enraptured television audience.

About surprises and phraseology, here's how it works. Or, more accurately, here's how it doesn't work when an interviewee becomes fixated by a question.

On May 26TH, 1974, a nice man by the name of Chesterfield Smith appeared as a guest on *Meet the Press*. At the time, Mr. Smith was President of the American Bar Association. Previously, the Chief Justice of the Supreme Court, Warren Burger, had made a speech in which he deplored widespread incompetency in the American bar. Naturally, because the speech was newsworthy, Mr. Burger's remarks were blazoned in the press from coast to coast and across the fruited plains. Even the people at NBC noticed them, including the reporter who was scheduled to interrogate Mr. Smith on *Meet the Press*.

It is probable that Mr. Smith also was aware of the Chief Justice's comments, although I don't know for sure because the ABA wasn't my client. Assuming that he did he might have anticipated a question about incompetency somewhere during the program, however that question might be posed.

Sure enough, he got one on the air, which was phrased exactly as follows:

REPORTER: Chief Justice Burger has complained at various times about the incompetency which can be found in the legal profession. What are the *odds* of ending up with a good lawyer for a middle-class American who is faced with a typical legal problem like divorce or an accident case?

Notice how the question turned on the word *odds*. Unfortunately for him, that seemed to mesmerize Mr. Smith. Maybe he forgot for an instant that he was the ABA President and not Jimmy the Greek, because in answering he did what comes all too naturally in polite society: he endeavored to plot the odds as he was asked. He said:

SMITH: There are lawyers in America who don't have the skills that I would like them to have. It's very difficult to identify them. It's very difficult to select the proper lawyer. I would say that the *odds* are about three to one that you'll get a very good lawyer if you don't work at it. But if you work at it, the odds are almost 100 percent that you can get a good lawyer.

As I mentioned, Mr. Smith seemed like a nice man, and I have no reason to conclude that he didn't speak the truth on *Meet the Press*. However, I would have cautioned him to remember two fundamental lessons: (1) beware of what comes all too naturally and (2) don't necessarily equate meeting the press with polite society. Mr. Smith's answer was both accommodating and compromising. At its core were two sentences in the middle, which many broadcasters decided to excerpt that very night on their news programs; they were the worst two sentences.

SMITH: It's very difficult to select the proper lawyer. I would say that the odds are about three to one that you'll get a very good lawyer if you don't work at it.

Hindsight is 20/20, and my intention here isn't to make fun of Chesterfield Smith for trashing his fellow lawyers. But in retrospect, and at the risk of my sounding like Jimmy the Greek, I'll bet another $50 that if Mr. Smith had blurted out the same reply in a practice session, the odds are better than three to one that he wouldn't have repeated it on the air.

Let me take a stab at writing down a preferable response for Mr. Smith, which is precisely what I want you to do between Friday and Sunday morning in constructing and composing those answers to the 25 questions that you expect on *Meet the Press*.

If we can safely presume that lawyers are fallible, then perhaps it follows that levels or degrees of competency and incompetency vary among them. If Mr. Smith was adamant about acknowledging that plain truth, okay. (I would have demurred on grounds that the point is too obvious to be newsworthy and certainly not helpful to the bar association's prestige.) Besides, that wasn't the question he was asked. In essence he was asked how a "middle-class American" can end up with "a good lawyer." Instead of digging himself a grave, why didn't he answer that question (and still be truthful)?

In concluding his response on *Meet the Press*, Mr. Smith said, "But if you work at it, the odds are almost 100 percent that you can get a good lawyer."

Let's start there with our new answer; in fact, let's start and finish it with words to that effect in the hope that viewers will remember them. Repetition is okay on television; it's even advised— preferably creative repetition, which is different from redundancy. (The oldest rule of education and/or advertising applies here: Tell them what you're going to tell them. Tell them. Then tell them what you told them.)

In between those two declarations by Mr. Smith, I would have suggested that he explain how a middle-class American might be advised to "work at it." Does he ask around for numerous recommendations? Does he visit several firms and interview the principals and other lawyers? Does he inquire if they have won similar cases? Does he ask for their references? And then check with those people? In short, before he puts his fate and perhaps his fortune in someone else's hands does he shop for a lawyer at least as much as he shops for neckties or a new carburetor?

That's good information, Mr. Smith. It's also helpful, maybe even interesting, and certainly truthful. Moreover, it doesn't denigrate the ABA membership that is paying you a salary, presumably to put the best possible face on their affairs and reputations.

So now we have the essence of a new answer about "incompetency," no matter how that question may be posed. It will fit as a response for any of the following.

> Mr. Smith, Warren Burger has mentioned that you and your fellow travelers are a bunch of jerks. Is he a jerk, too?

Or:

> Mr. Smith, the Chief Justice was musing the other day that most of you guys should be disbarred and incarcerated. How would you feel about a little jail time?

Or:

> Mr. Smith, one of your peers said the other night in a speech that the American people would be better represented in legal matters by a street vendor with a monkey on a chain. He's right, isn't he?

I'm trying to make this as nasty and difficult as possible in our practice session, which is far more rigorous than anyone would expect on a responsible program like *Meet the Press*. And I would counsel Mr. Smith to reply the same way to any of the above, as follows:

> The Chief Justice and I are completely in accord about what we want for the American people—competent legal advice and assistance. And if a client *works at it,* the odds are virtually 100 percent that he can get a fine lawyer. Get recommendations. Visit the firms and interview. Check references. Shopping like he does for anything assures a client the services of a brilliant lawyer. (Or words to that effect.)

Now I dare the nightly newscasts to emasculate that comment or make my new client, Mr. Smith, look like a dunce.

The first sentence in our revised answer is clearly a preface, not the guts of it, and if a newscast chooses to omit it due to time constraints, okay (although I prefer otherwise because picking a fight with the Chief Justice of the Supreme Court isn't high on my client's list of objectives). The central message for our side commences in the second sentence, after the word *and*. I'd advise Mr. Smith to pause briefly after *and*, and attack the word *if*, as if the sentence started as follows: "If a client works at it...."

If Mr. Smith had done thusly on *Meet the Press* in 1974, we might have seen the following excerpt on the nightly TV news:

> If a client works at it, the odds are virtually 100 percent that he can get a fine lawyer. Get recommendations. Visit the firms and interview. Check references. (Notice the short sentences and plain English, also aiding comprehension and retention.) Shopping like he does for anything assures a client the services of a brilliant lawyer.

Bullseye! Forty three words, which is a perfect fit for television news. And in those 43 words the emphasis is shifted from the incompetency of lawyers to the responsibilities of their intended clients; hopefully building a successful bridge.

The defense rests.

Now let's move to the other side of the ledger, the offensive game plan for Sunday, and when we're finished I want you to put the two plans side by side on the kitchen table. You may be startled to notice how well they match and correlate with each other. That's because you and the reporter(s) on *Meet the Press* are interested in, and will be talking about, the same topic(s), although you may view and address them from diametrically opposite directions. That's why you were invited in the first place. Presumably you have knowledge, insight, experience, authority, involvement, culpability, or expertise concerning whatever the hell we're talking about here, and they want to get to the bottom of it.

However, don't think because you've plotted 25 likely questions that you're now obliged to list 25 topics or statements of your own (unless you happen to be very pushy and an exceedingly fast talker). That's what I meant when I told the college presidents: "Don't be greedy, but you're certainly entitled to ventilate a few items of your own, not necessarily in response to someone else's questions."

In the same article, I also advised the academic types to:

1) *Be enthusiastic.* Not like a cheerleader. Conviction is what I'm talking about, and you convey conviction to a television audience through the vitality and intensity of your presentation. If you don't seem convinced, you won't convince us either.

2) *Be specific.* We, the general public, are a dispassionate audience, and there are certain points you want us to remember when *Meet the Press* ends. So fix those points in our minds vividly, colorfully and, as a result, memorably.
   Also, something isn't so just because you say it's so. We're not the freshman class. Back up assertions with facts, examples, statistics, and even pertinent personal experiences.

3) *Be correct.* Being correct comes from being prepared. Being incorrect about one little thing, if you're called on it, can undermine your credibility in toto (as President Reagan occasionally demonstrates).

4) *Be anecdotal.* As they say at *ABC Sports*, TV is "up close and personal." Use it that way. You're not addressing both houses of Congress on *Meet the Press*. You're in a living room with a few friends. Don't pontificate and declaim. Tell us stories in everyday language.

5) *Be cool.* Few TV encounters will be confrontational, but heated discussions aren't unprecedented. Don't you get heated, however. Audiences usually side with the more composed of the combatants. Joseph P. Kennedy once said (or frequently said): "Don't get mad, get even." Mahatma Gandhi said it even better: "When you're in the right, you can afford to keep your temper. When you're in the wrong, you can't afford to lose it."

Jot down in the offense column the three things that you definitely want to say on *Meet the Press*. Simple, declarative sentences will suffice for now.

Write the same points a second time expressed another way.

Now a third time, again differently.

Voila! In all probability, we've now got nine statements or assertions on three separate (or even related) themes.

But as I mentioned, those of us in your TV audience, particularly the reporters on *Meet the Press*, are from Missouri. It's time for you to put up or shut up. Prove the assertions.

Does a revered and beloved expert agree with you? If so write down his or her comments and testimony underneath one of your statements, along with a short list of that person's impeccable credentials and distinctions.

Are the statistics and data overwhelmingly in your favor? Cite them under another assertion—carefully, correctly, and completely.

Did a similar thing happen previously? If it supports your contention, tell us the experience (first in writing on your ledger); also remind us that if we don't remember history, we're probably doomed to repeat it.

Is this issue like some other issue? Are the two matters analogous? Explain the analogy.

Did you see it for yourself, firsthand? Tell us what you saw.

Do the facts underscore your case? I mean "the *true* facts," as President Eisenhower used to say (presumably as opposed to someone else's untrue facts). If so, lay them on us.

Keep doing this until you have nine different, supportive dissertations, attaching one to each of your declarations.

You have just diagrammed and choreographed the whole conversation on next Sunday's *Meet the Press* program, and the two sides of your ledger should fairly well match each other (unless by chance Marvin Kalb wants to inquire about your recent pilgrimage to Afghanistan and you want to discuss root canal therapy).

Now, with the teeniest amount of bridging and oral dexterity, and in the total absence of fixation, can't you respond to the 25 likely questions with any or parts of these nine recitations? (If not, start over, because if you're doing this correctly the answer will always be yes.)

As previously noted, the route from defense (questions) to offense (statements and support) is called bridging.

For example, on the occasion of his retirement after three decades of fine service at *NBC News*, Edwin Newman was interviewed by a colleague.

REPORTER: Ed, can you point to a "finest program" in your long career?

NEWMAN: I can't do that. (Here comes the *bridge*.) But I can tell you what exhilarates me the most about our business. It's the emergencies. . . .

If you watch television attentively (which few viewers do, partly explaining why this tactic is so successful), you will see demonstrations of the bridging technique on virtually every program.

I *can't* tell you *that*. But I *can* tell you *this*.

It works for two reasons: the guest is willing (and prepared) to take the initiative by volunteering new information about a topic, hopefully more interesting or provocative information than the question seemed to elicit.

Bridging is a basic trick in this trade, which was adapted from debating techniques. It springs from the ground of common sense and basically boils down to a single premise: never let the host or other participants control your contribution to the program; reserve that privilege for yourself.

The best guests don't evade the difficult questions. Only novices try that, and most are trampled in the ensuing pursuit. If you evade a question, it will probably be asked again. If you evade again, attention will be focused on your evasiveness, which is exactly what you don't want.

But an accomplished interviewee knows that it is possible to restructure a question before answering it and in so doing to remove the worst dangers. If it is done skillfully enough, it may be possible not to answer the question at all without looking evasive.

An accomplished guest volunteers much more than the required information when he or she likes a question. When a question is too delicate, or tangential, or petty the same guest volunteers nothing. No question is sacred, and none need be answered slavishly. That's how amateurs get caught. You are entitled to say everything you choose to say about all the topics that are raised, whether the initiative was somebody else's or your own. You do not need to answer specific questions.

Through this tactic, as I said, it is possible, even likely, for an interviewee to actually control the conversational exchanges.

The time has come for me to bridge to the next chapter, as follows:

REPORTER: Mr. Hilton, how does a person prepare for an appearance on *Meet the Press?*

HILTON: Preparation is essential, but performance is more important on television because style predominates over substance....

chapter five
Style versus Substance

On the left was John F. Kennedy in a dark suit, sporting a deep tan.

On the right was Richard M. Nixon looking emaciated, pale, and perspiring.

The occasion, in 1960, was the first presidential debate in television history, which took place at WBBM-TV in Chicago (where I worked at the time).

Vaguely I recall a bit of bickering between the two men about Quemoy and Matsu, tiny rock-pile islands off the coast of mainland China (which President Nixon flew over in the early 1970s en route to Peking). But mostly I remember that CBS's paint job on the back walls of the stage area had dried a lighter shade of gray than Nixon's minions had expected. It closely matched the color of the Vice President's suit, rendering him next to invisible. (Some of you also may recall black and white television, which prevailed in 1960.) Mr. Kennedy wore a dark blue suit which may have been too dark for color TV. But in black and white he seemed crisper than Mr. Nixon, and bolder by comparison.

The contrast in skin tones was likewise stark: Kennedy was richly tanned (as always) having campaigned outdoors the week before in southern California; Mr. Nixon was pallid, recently ill, and showing it. The Vice President nevertheless refused the application of makeup (which would have evened the score) because Mr. Kennedy had declined. The difference was that Kennedy didn't need it.

I bring this up because appearances and otherwise extraneous or seemingly superficial and cosmetic things like wardrobes and complexions take on disproportionate importance on television, which is a point to remember as you prepare for Sunday's *Meet the Press*.

For instance, I've occasionally wondered in retrospect if Mr. Nixon might have won that night if somehow he had stanched his eccrine glands. Instead, he perspired freely under the hot lights, appearing ineffectual, tentative, haunted, and intimidated. Mr. Kennedy seemed assured, confident, and assertive. (Perspiring, incidentally, is another problem that television makeup can mitigate by somewhat closing and clogging the pores.)

Also in retrospect (and with the possible exceptions of Quemoy and Matsu), I can hardly recall a remark of significance from either candidate in their unprecedented confrontation. But my impressions and remembrances of the two men have lasted indelibly for more than a quarter-century. (That is one of the reasons why I persist in my contention that impressions outweigh substance on television; manner has more impact than matter on a TV audience.)

One of my recollections from 1960 is that Kennedy addressed us on television; Mr. Nixon addressed the issues of the day and scored forensic points. Most people who listened on radio, who were denied the visuals and forced to concentrate on the substance of the words, thought Nixon did the better job. However, most Americans watched on television and concluded the opposite.

Years later Mr. Nixon had learned his lesson. "Rely totally on your television producer," he said in an interview advising other presidential aspirants. "Let him put on makeup, even though you hate it. Let him tell you how to sit. Let him tell you what your best camera angles are. Let him tell you what to do with your hair.

"You know," said Mr. Nixon, "it must turn people off to think that you've got to go to the barber and get your hair blown dry, and then fixed just properly and everything in place. But that's the television age. And it turns *me* off. But having been burned once by not doing it, I never made that mistake again. And I would urge all prospective candidates in the future, be sure you remember that more important than what you say is how you *look* on television."

Deplore it if you want, but style always predominates over content on television. There is no way for a viewer to stop a discussion or interview in progress while he or she reasons through an argument, so in the end the audience's reaction to the participants in a dialogue on television is overwhelmingly emotional, and less intellectual.[1]

In books, magazines, and newspapers what is said is usually more important than how it is said. On television, as Mr. Nixon observed, just the opposite is true. In radio the absence of visual stimulus and distraction permits a listener to concentrate on the content or substance. But on television, seeing an interviewee who is confused or exasperated, groping for words or perspiring heavily, supersedes any statement, and the total impression of a personality is what's left.

As I concede about my recollections of Kennedy versus Nixon in 1960, the emotional content of a program will remain in a viewer's memory far longer than any ideas expressed. If you are very lucky, a viewer might remember one point that you make on an interview show, particularly one made dramatically, colorfully, or righteously. And even after that has faded from memory, the personal impression remains. Mostly a viewer will remember whether or not you are likable; that's all. And that is why losing your temper or lowering yourself to the level of a rude host or a swinish fellow panelist is among the worst of offenses. (Remember: Be cool!)

Two examples come instantly to mind: the first is about memorability, the second about impressions.

---

[1] Increasingly, Americans are purchasing videocassette recorders (known in the trade as VCRs) for their homes. So if a program is taped, it can be stopped and started in the replaying of it. However, I don't know anyone who does it (except me, and only rarely). Also, a few newspapers, notably *The New York Times*, print entire transcripts of speeches and proceedings, usually involving the president of the United States and comparable luminaries. Whether they're widely read is another matter.

On the day after the Reagan–Carter TV debate in 1980, and subsequently, the most-repeated, most-remembered comment by either candidate was "There you go again!" Yet no one in my poll on the next morning, and since, could remember (1) what provoked it or (2) what Mr. Reagan said thereafter. (Mostly my respondents thought Reagan had won the Carter debate because they *liked* him better than the incumbent President.)

More recently, early in the Democratic primary campaign of 1984 when Gary Hart's popularity had reached its zenith, people on the eastern seaboard, most of whom had seen the Colorado Senator only on television, were asked by pollsters why they liked him. Most responded in terms of Mr. Hart's "freshness," "appearance," and "youth." These *impressions* of the candidate translated into votes in places like New Hampshire, Florida, Massachusetts, and Rhode Island, among others. (A few people mentioned Hart's "new ideas," but hardly anyone was specific on that score.)

The same Gary Hart, the prime beneficiary of TV exposure in the late winter and early spring of 1984, previously expressed awe and apprehension about "the incredible power of television" in 1972. After he witnessed it at close range as George McGovern's campaign manager, he said to a Chicago newspaper columnist, "It's a very frightening thing. A Hitler, a dictator, *could rise* in a matter of a few days with the proper use of TV."

In a radio commentary at the time I concurred with the Senator, and said, "One of the problems is that *images* of the candidates and snappy *one-liners* or *quips* work best on TV, neither having much or anything to do with how a president will govern us, or act in office. That's because campaigning in the television age is largely sloganeering. It's also why an *informed* voter needs more than television to make an educated choice, despite TV's unparalleled powers of transmission. Unfortunately, few of us commit the necessary time, so, instead of voting intelligently, we more often vote emotionally. And that's a scenario for someday putting the wrong person in the White House."

I contend on the same basis that TV debates for presidential candidates are paradoxical at best. Staged for television, which is, frankly, a theatrical mass medium, the likely winner in the collective opinion of a dispassionate audience is inevitably the candidate who best exhibits quick-wittedness, which I argue is the diametric opposite of what we seek from a chief executive. No, mental acuity isn't exactly a minus for a debater, but, given the choice, wouldn't we prefer a president to be deliberative and thoughtful? Pondering the questions at length, carefully evaluating the options and alternatives, is what I hope a president actually does in office. However, demonstrating that prowess in a TV debate will surely prompt an audience to conclude that non compos mentis is advancing.

Having raised the spectrum of likability, let me elaborate for purposes of your appearance on *Meet the Press*. In fact, the first two of my precepts and suggestions for successful performances on television are (1) be yourself and (2) be liked (a mutually exclusive feat for a number of politicians with whom I have worked).

I explained as follows in my magazine article for the college presidents:

> *Be yourself.* Put on airs and a TV audience will see through you like an X-ray machine. President Lyndon Johnson, an earthy wheeler-dealer in private, concluded (perhaps correctly) that his real persona wasn't sufficiently *presidential* for public consumption. So he assumed a de Gaulle-like pose on TV—and frequently came across like the droning narrator of a third-rate historical pageant. LBJ was playing a role, not being himself (whereas "spokesmanship," fundamentally, is an *extension* of *self*).
>
> *Be liked.* Two of your role models could be the late President Kennedy for his grace and wit (occasionally self-depreciating), and President Reagan for his warmth and affability. If your TV audience likes you, it may listen to you more closely and be more inclined to accept what you say—even agree with you. If your audience doesn't like you, the steel curtain slams down.

Likability can be achieved, even if you've never won a popularity contest. You may be likable because you came well prepared and backed up your statements with crisp, specific examples or well-researched statistics. You may be likable because you showed great humor or composure in the face of adversity (even though you failed to score any of the points which you intended). You may be likable because you became an underdog at the mercy of a bullying host. You can fail to state any of your objectives and still win as long as the viewer at home feels admiration or sympathy for you.

But your attitude can work against you, too. If you look bored by the questions, are arrogant in refusing to defend or explain your position clearly, imply that the program didn't warrant preparation, or appear to relish the humiliation of a fellow guest whose position you don't countenance, you risk losing everything you hoped to gain. You may actually be in the right about certain points, but your style has defeated you.

Likability in some respects has replaced all other measures for the effective use of television. The Q rating system, which ranks performers by their likability (and familiarity) quotient, explains why a number of television personalities have been given the chance to fail more than once. If a performer does well in the Q ratings, he or she will be paraded out on program after program until the right vehicle can be found.

In short, if your name or face conjures up warm feelings of friendliness in a viewer, you are doing your job on television (even if you have nothing to say and couldn't make a point on a pencil with an electric sharpener).

To be liked on television requires the mastery of only a few fundamental principles. Roone Arledge at ABC-TV gets credit for that "up-close and personal" line in promoting his network's sports coverage. More scholarly were Marshall McLuhan's references to television as the "cool" medium, meaning it works best if it's used intimately, conversationally, "up-close and personally."

One of the keys to intimacy and closeness is eye contact with the camera's lens, which is tantamount to eye contact with the audience at home. Ronald Reagan didn't know you personally when he was the Republican candidate for president in 1980, but he spoke to you personally at the conclusion of his TV debate with

Jimmy Carter when he said, "Next Tuesday is Election Day. Next Tuesday all of you will go to the polls." (Note again the repetition and short sentences.) "You'll stand there in the polling place and make a decision. I think when you make that decision, it might be well if you ask yourself, are you better off than you were four years ago?"

Ignoring a vast congregation of persons in the Cleveland auditorium, Mr. Reagan spoke those lines directly, conversationally, and earnestly to you at home. And all the while he looked at you, too.

McLuhan was the first person to refer to television as the "cool" medium and, after the general election of 1984, Walter Mondale admitted he never "warmed up" to it—a revealing dichotomy of terms. In fact, the former Vice President was generally too hot to be successful on television, mostly a reference to his tone.

Lest we get bogged down in temperature metaphors, let me explain.

At a political rally of 10,000 fanatical supporters, persons in the audience are apt to be seated (if they're seated at all) at a considerable distance from the principal speaker. Moreover, those persons are likely to be passionate observers who are involved and participating in the event. To rouse such an audience to the desired frenzy, a candidate is advised to be *declamatory* ("vehement oratory, loudly demanding attention") in his speech, which is hopefully a turn-on for such a crowd. (That's what is meant by *hot*.)

Seeing the same candidate on television is a different phenomenon, however. Audiences are less frenzied, in fact, they are mostly dispassionate, and dispersed in millions of homes, watching singly or in small groups and sitting 12 to 15 feet from a TV set. To be shouted at from that distance is more likely a turn-off for most of us. We prefer to be addressed conversationally, coolly. (Throughout his public career, Mr. Mondale rarely made that distinction, resultantly appearing somewhat shrill on television.)

These principles apply to you on *Meet the Press*, although you're probably not a candidate to lead the Free World. As the diagram shows, you and your interlocutors will face each other at perhaps a distance of six or eight feet. Somewhere behind you, probably over your left shoulder, will be a camera for them. Although the back of your head and left shoulder may be seen in the foreground of some of its pictures, that camera isn't for you; it primarily takes the pictures of Marvin Kalb and his fellow reporter(s), so forget about it. Perpendicular to your left and the panel's right will be another camera. This one is the one least used on the program. It provides the cover shots (in television jargon), which are pictures of you and the reporters in profile seated across from each other; this is probably the picture that will be seen at the beginning and end of the program. (At the end the stage lights may be faded down so the participants will appear in silhouette on home TV screens.) Forget about that camera, too.

"Meet the Press"

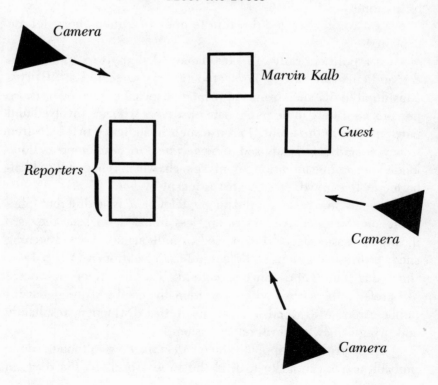

The one for you will be positioned somewhere behind the panel, perhaps between the interviewers, at a distance of 15 to 20 feet from your chair. For you, that camera is the American people—maybe 5,000,000 of them in half that many homes "watching singly or in small groups, sitting 12 to 15 feet" from their television sets. But don't be intimidated (something else, I admit, that is easier said than done). They can see you (up-close and personally), but you can't see them, which helps for openers.

Moreover, don't think of them as a mass of 5,000,000 people, because those of us who watch the program at home are unaware and apathetic about the rest of your audience. As I view your performance on Sunday, it won't occur to me (and even if it did, I couldn't care less) that 5,000,000 of my fellow citizens are likewise watching in condominiums from Miami to Seattle, in rural towns throughout the Great Plains, in the adobe dwellings of the Southwest, and the rustic villages in New England. I'm at home alone in my den. It's midday on a Sunday. I've finished the papers, but probably not the coffee. And all I want is to eavesdrop on a stimulating, fascinating, provocative, and topical conversation.

So that camera in front of you *isn't* 5,000,000 people anymore. It's me. (It's your spouse, your next-door neighbor, your best friend— any *one* of us.) And although you're ensconced in a studio in Washington, D.C., I'm not hundreds or thousands of miles away from you. I'm across the room in my den (not your television studio). Just talk to me with that in mind, even glance my way when you think it's appropriate.

I'll like you better.

As I observe you (up-close and personally) I'm apt to notice your posture, your wardrobe, certainly your general appearance, your facial expressions, your gestures, which are aspects of a comparatively superficial nature for me to like or not. I'll particularly notice if any of these strike me as odd or somehow wrong. If they are, at worst, I'll think less of you; at best, I'll be distracted from what you are saying. Don't let that happen.

Be comfortable in your chair, but not too comfortable. Don't let me surmise that you were dumped into it from an altitude of 1,500 feet. Sit up, cross your legs, lean slightly forward (toward me), and keep your hands in front of you above your waist. Even use your hands to punctuate your points (like you probably do in everyday conversations). Just remember one thing. The picture of you that I see at home, at least most of the time, is bounded horizontally by the approximate width of your shoulders. Vertically it's from the top of your head to your sternum, maybe to your waist.

Grand gestures work like a charm in a huge auditorium. Small gestures work on TV, keeping your hands in front of your upper torso, but not in front of your face, please.

And about that garishly plaid sports jacket, the one that reminds everyone of Nathan Detroit: don't wear it on Sunday (unless you happen to be a tout by profession, and your mission on *Meet the Press* is to promote off-track betting). In fact, don't wear anything so flashy that it draws my attention. You want us to be engrossed by you, not your packaging.

Midtone clothing is the best: blues, grays, and browns. (Black should be avoided because it absorbs too much light, adding to the appearance of tonnage on camera.) Men should be sure to wear knee-length socks. No exceptions. And the socks should be darker than the suit.

Always keep a double-breasted jacket buttoned. You may unbutton a single-breasted coat, but you should keep it fairly well in front of you. Don't let it flop open too wide.

Wear only one patterned item, and make sure it's a fairly quiet pattern. If your tie is patterned, wear a solid shirt and preferably a solid suit. Avoid tightly-patterned tweeds and herringbones. They have a tendency to *moire* (the appearance of waviness or movement, an optical illusion that makes a pattern look strangely animated) on television.

The rules against busy-looking clothing apply to women, too, but their problems are more complex. Find out the color of the set. One guest on the *Today Show* planned to wear a snappy designer suit in bright red for her appearance. The set was bright orange. You are always safe with neutral colors: blue, varying shades of gray, brown, or khaki.

Try to avoid wearing something new but, if you must, test if first by sitting in a chair in front of a mirror. Does it add twenty pounds when you sit down? Is your skirt long enough to keep you modest, no matter how heated the discussion? Try the chair trick with an older outfit, too. Occasionally what you feel comfortable in looks terrible, but being in a familiar dress or suit relieves some of the burden of the experience. It's one less thing to worry about.

Prints with a pattern that includes flowers, geometric forms, animals, or other recognizable objects in a size larger than an inch square are best avoided. Viewers will watch the dress instead of you.

Don't overdress or underdress. Clothing you would expect to see on a bank vice president will do you at any hour. Men should get no more casual than a sports jacket (sans garish) in lieu of a suit. Women, while they need not wear a formal suit of the sort John T. Molloy recommends for successful dress, should wear a skirt rather than a pantsuit if they are not of perfect figure. The skirt may be a suit with a jacket or a dress, but it should fall in that same range of muted colors mentioned before. If it's an evening show, a long skirt and sweater or tailored jacket are fine. In the afternoon, a long skirt looks out of place—people will think you're on the way to a cocktail party. (In the morning, they'll think you've just left the party, and your coherency will be questioned.)

A word about jewelry. Wedding rings and watches are fine, but anything else requires close scrutiny. Jangly bracelets are out, and chains or necklaces are appropriate only if the wearer is sure they will not clunk against a lavaliere microphone (or make any sort of independent noise a microphone may pick up). Be prepared to take off at the last moment any jewelry that might interfere.

On eyeglasses: If you wear them ordinarily, wear them on television. (Be yourself!) Try not to wear chrome or shiny metal frames, however, because they can catch light and flare. To be especially secure, move the bows slightly up off your ears (provided you have sufficient hair to cover them). This angles the lenses down a bit as insurance against glare from the lights on the set. (The best frames are very thin tortoise shell.)

While we're discussing general appearances, let's dispense with cosmetics, too.

Network shows and the larger stations in major cities always have someone on hand to help a guest with makeup if you choose to avail yourself of that service. (Others do not, so it is best to assume that no makeup will be available in most small stations.) TV makeup, unlike stage or street makeup, is not used for dramatic effect on a program such as *Meet the Press*. It has a very practical purpose: it prevents the strong studio lights from using your face as a reflector. Without makeup, the lights have a tendency to bounce off a face with an unpleasant shine. A touch of pancake, however, lets your face absorb the light, giving you a smoother, more natural look.

If you ordinarily wear pancake makeup, just put it on carefully and, if you don't usually wear it, summon up your courage and ask for help at a cosmetics counter. Ask for a pancake to suit your coloring. Testing it on the back of the hand is standard procedure. Look for a color as close to your own skin tone as possible, cheating toward a slightly darker shade if you can't get an exact match. Buy an applicator sponge, too, and some cream or lotion for removing makeup, unless the brand you choose is water soluble.

Then practice at home, whether or not you ordinarily wear makeup. If you are lucky enough to have access to a videotape camera for rehearsal, by all means wear your makeup for that. Dab on a light coating, covering all the exposed skin, including the backs of your hands (which we'll also see as you gesture). Many people make the mistake of putting on too much makeup, which is as bad as no makeup at all, because your skin takes on a chalky, one-color effect that looks very artificial. If you can see no gradation in your skin tone after applying makeup, you have too much on.

Men: if the top of your head is bald, cover it all. (Bald women should avoid television.) If your hairline is receding, make sure you apply the makeup into the hairline, not just across the middle of the forehead; also down to the collar on your neck. If you don't do that, blend it under your jaw so there is no line of demarcation. Women should extend the makeup down under the neckline of the dress or suit. A partial makeup job can be worse than no makeup at all, because you'll look as if you have a mask on.

Whatever the fashion on the street, women should beware of the bold rouged look. Simply wear enough blusher to give a slightly rosy tone across the cheekbones, and make sure that it blends imperceptibly into the cheek near the hairline. Lipstick should not be a vivid shade of red, but one of the muted, dusty tones. Don't wear lip gloss. Instead, if you wish, finish your lips with a dusting powder, and make sure you have applied and blotted enough layers of lipstick to last throughout the show. If you can't be sure, you'd be wise to forego all but the most minimal lip treatment.

Eyelashes, if false, should look real. If you can put your face four inches from an illuminated makeup mirror without destroying the illusion, your eyelashes are okay. The same goes for mascara. There should be no lumps, no noticeable stiffness, from four inches.

Women who are very skillful with makeup may wish to sculpt their faces subtly for the camera. A layer of light-colored blemish eraser applied sparingly below the eye (but just to the bottom edge of the eyesocket, please) will mask bags and wrinkles. Eye shadow should be equally light, almost imperceptible, with a light color under the brows, a darker brown, mauve, or other neutral color on the lids. To thin the face, suck in your cheeks and apply a tiny bit of taupe or mauve eye shadow in the hollow, blending it to near invisibility. This accents the cheekbones and minimizes the jaw. Finally, apply a little blusher down the bridge of your nose and on the tip of your chin. When you're through, only the differences in skin tone should be visible, not the cosmetics used to achieve them.

Topping off this fussiness is a word about your hair. (Bald readers may skip to the next chapter. I'll join you there in a moment.)

Men should avoid the wet look. Visit a barber on Thursday or Friday before Sunday's *Meet the Press*. (Neatness counts unless you're Don King or Boy George.) Then wash your hair again on Saturday morning, and on Sunday morning, too—except if you have hair like mine which is completely unmanageable for a minimum of 24 hours.

Remember that while the makeup artists at NBC may give your face a once-over, they're not running a beauty parlor. Coiffing is done for their people, not you. Coif yourself in front of a mirror before the program starts, and wear your glasses during the process. Don't put them on at the last minute.

Women should keep it simple and, for most of you, not severe. If your face is smashing, if the years have yet to take their toll, you might opt for something close-cropped or sleek, like a turban or a chignon. Otherwise you should experiment with softer hair styles that complement the contours of your face.

If your hair is long, anchor it somehow on the sides so it doesn't cascade across your face. Ears aren't the best anchors, incidentally (unless yours are unusually large). If your hair isn't secured you are apt to spend 30 minutes fiddling with it on-camera, which is another unnecessary distraction for viewers.

And please pay heed as we begin this flight to what I said about the television camera as an X-ray machine. If that switch doesn't exactly match your natural hair, or if those roots are darker than the rest of your tresses, you will appear on *Meet the Press* in two-tone. Even the subtleties become brazenly obvious on a studio set.

I have been a private pilot for 20 years and, using the parlance of air traffic controllers, I now proclaim you cleared for take-off with Marvin Kalb. It's remarkable! In a mere five chapters you have matriculated from nowhere to a network television debut. Congratulations.

However, don't think ground school is entirely over. A number of the basics for meeting the press have yet to be reviewed.

chapter six
Basic Training

It is necessary to disabuse some old canards about press relations that you may hold to be self-evident.

Especially since Watergate, and really since the era of the so-called muckrakers, it has been insufficient to communicate publicly by means of those carefully-tweezed written statements known as press releases or through a surrogate, unless you happen to be the president of the United States. (Even presidents are flushed into public view, unshielded by intermediaries, on occasion.) That blanket statement fairly well covers the 20TH century since Teddy Roosevelt first referred to certain reporters as muckrakers in 1906. (It's another of those old-fashioned English words that most of us don't use in everyday conversations. But don't bother looking it up. To *muckrake* is "to search for and expose political or commercial corruption." The best way to avoid muckraking is not to be corrupt in the first place.)

At worst, press releases arriving at thousands of newsrooms in the morning mail are deposited in the trash unread or unopened. At best they are noted before a reporter calls you on the phone in search of further information. If a surrogate takes the call, that person will be perceived as a conduit, a facilitator of the ultimate interview with you, not as a substitute, although surrogates usually are questioned, too.

Once there was a legendary public relations man in America by the name of Ivy Lee, who worked most notably for John D. Rockefeller. While the patriarch dispensed shiny dimes to urchins on street corners, Mr. Lee dispensed information to the press about the Standard Oil Trust and his employer's philanthropy. Inevitably there was more news about the latter than the former.

In fact, Mr. Lee was a nearly unbreachable barrier between Rockefeller and the press, and reporters were restricted to a diet of informational table scraps in lieu of feasts.

Nowadays, the press's appetite is more voracious and insatiable. Although the First Amendment to the U.S. Constitution was adopted in 1791, it wasn't until later that it became so liberally and aggressively interpreted by some reporters.

The right to know is stridently claimed by today's free press, especially the public's right to know, although neither is specifically delineated in the Bill of Rights. These rights to know are most frequently invoked in contacts with public officials, where the best supportive case can be made in a pluralistic and democratic society. As a result, a remark by Joe Louis in the 1940s about challenger Billy Conn can be applied to most any public figure as the 20TH century draws to a close: "He can run. But he can't hide."

Today's reporters are unlikely to accept an Ivy Lee intermediary instead of a principal, resulting in the mismatches that this book fundamentally addresses: professional interrogators versus amateur respondents. No chief executive officer with whom I have worked has been formally schooled or highly experienced in press relations. Mostly they slog their ways to the top by other avenues (lawyering, sales, finance, business administration, and so on) and upon arrival in the corner office, the mantle of spokesmanship is instantaneously conferred (notwithstanding the availability of an aide-de-camp in an adjoining suite with Ivy Lee's skills and credentials).

It's true, however, that every prospective interviewee has the right to remain silent, because the Fifth Amendment is applicable, too (not to mention the Eighth). But also understand the consequences of that course.

In an article for that paragon of scholarship known as *Penthouse* magazine, author Michael Korda once advised that "when talking to the media, the most important words to remember are *no comment.*" A jaded public relations man by the name of Victor Gold concurs, although I am inclined to dismiss him as an expert because he formerly worked for Spiro Agnew. Writing in *The Washingtonian,* Mr. Gold said, "If Mike Wallace calls, hang up!"

Hanging up is another of your inalienable rights under the U.S. Constitution because Wallace, unlike Congress and the courts, lacks subpoena power. If you consent to an interview there may be unpleasant consequences, yes. And ditto, more surely, if you don't consent, please remember.

Hanging up on Mike Wallace is apt to result in his arriving with a *60 Minutes* crew on your doorstep to deliver a diatribe on-camera about the man or woman inside (POINTING) who refuses to talk to us! His audience, perhaps approximating 10 to 15 percent of the entire U.S. population for a given program, is therefore likely to conclude that the cowering one is admittedly guilty of heinous and reprehensible crimes. (*No comment* sends roughly the same signal.)

Even if that doesn't happen, Mr. Wallace is almost certain (probably with renewed vigor and commitment) to concoct and assemble his report about you anyway (now without your participation and input) leaving disproportionate time on network television for your many detractors and accusers. (Don't forget, TV news is principally an arena for conflict, as previously stated.)

If either of those eventualities strike you as acceptable, hang up on Mike Wallace when he calls.

But I am not writing this book to scare the daylights out of you about the press. Quite the contrary. And please recall my central thesis as you turn these pages: it is altogether possible to *succeed* in a press interview, or at least to survive. I can think of no greater disservice for me to perform (a la Korda and Gold) than to increase your anxiety and apprehension. My goal is the opposite.

You may be wondering at this point how to become newsworthy, if you aren't already. Oftentimes the press will find you. If you were the victim of a spectacular hijacking or disaster; if you're a banker, and one of your tellers has embezzled a six-figure sum; if you're a broker who has spent the last five years kiting checks, television and the press will make room for your face either locally or nationally. Sometimes you don't have any choice.

But when you are trying to make the news, it's you who decides when to call for press attention, and shortly I will explain a few of the ways.

First the basics.

Good press relations are constant; faulty press relations are intermittent or infrequent. A mistake often made is to shun the press between crises, meaning reporters see you only when something is amiss, at which time you are complete strangers. Contrary to the adage, familiarity does not breed contempt unless you happen to be contemptible. Things like circumscription and disdain are more likely to breed the contempt of reporters (or at least their suspicion), meaning the press is more inclined to assume a measure of culpability on your part from the first notification or occurrence of a problem. That tends to make your task an uphill struggle, whereas ideally you should seek a level playing field for these encounters. (Downhill is even more fun.)

Other views are often expressed, but the best reporters are fair. Most reporters are fair. They're also human. If you've been square with them in the past, forthcoming and candid, they'll be inclined toward open-mindedness when you're in (as George Bush says) "deep do-do," provided your version of events also is plausible and complete. (Taking a liberty with the language, the accepted definition of the word *corollary* is "a proposition that follows with little or no proof *from one already proven.*" In my adaptation, the proven one, on the basis of past experiences and contacts with reporters, should be you, not another proposition.)

Most of us don't hesitate to turn our backs to a friend or acquaintance on a darkened street, but we won't do the same to a suspicious stranger, which is my definition of *wary.* So you as a stranger to the press are likely to be perceived warily, notwithstanding your Ph.D. degree from Princeton, your four-star rank in the military, your impeccable record as a public official, or your CEO title with a major corporation.

By nature, most reporters are populists (with a small p). They think of themselves as representatives of the people. They are apt to prefer Davids to Goliaths, so a Ph.D. degree, a four-star rank, an impeccable record, and a CEO title can add steepness to the incline in an uphill struggle.

No, that part isn't fair. But it's true, and it's human nature. Reporters think: the bigger they are, the harder they fall, and the more rewarding it is to topple them.

Woodward and Bernstein nailed Richard Nixon, became famous, and made millions. Applications from high school seniors to journalism schools surged in the middle 1970s. Something called investigative reporting came into vogue. Investigative reporting is a ridiculous misnomer because all reporting, by nature and definition, is investigative, at least to some extent. (That's why you're apt to be called on the phone by a reporter, who has gotten your press release, who wants to check it out, to probe more deeply, and so on.)

Clones of Woodward and Bernstein are currently stationed in America's press rooms. In the future, a water commissioner may fall, perhaps another president. Meantime, you will do nicely, thanks.

And fall you might if you haven't been straight in the past; if you've previously disdained reporters because you thought you didn't need them, especially when they thought they needed you.

Accommodation is a good rule to play by, although I'm not suggesting that you're always obliged to meet the press. There are exceptions to every rule and, in rare circumstances, it is advisable to demur. (For instance, President Nixon frequently demurred and was secluded during the Watergate siege. Aides-de-camp didn't demur. At last, although the press wasn't wholly responsible, many of the latter went to federal penitentiaries. Mr. Nixon went to San Clemente.)

Finally on the basics list, reporters are curious and inquisitive. Otherwise they wouldn't hold reporting jobs. As previously revealed, they are trained from puberty to ask everyone who, what, when, where, why, and how? Your job is to answer them succinctly and truthfully, which is a job made appreciably easier in a crisis if reporters already know from past contacts *who* you are, *what* you do, and *where* and *why.* That leaves *when* and *how?* This makes for a more level playing field in moments of stress when the press is hurried and you are harassed.

Most reporters read hugely to sate their native curiosities, so even if you're a stranger at the time of your first encounter they probably know a lot about you and from whence you came. (Nor do reporters consider themselves limited to a single topic during an interview with you, even a so-called crisis interview. They are frequently inclined to explore other matters, which you may regard as irrelevant or extraneous. We'll deal with that in the next chapter.)

So much for a miniprofile of reporters in America. How to appeal to them is the next order of business and, especially for purposes of television, some things are easier to sell than others. If you are promoting a worthy cause with a hot-air balloon race, all you have to do is alert the assignment desks at the local stations and there will be a cavalry charge of reporters and crews to get there early for the best camera positions. The same is true of a kite fly, an egg roll, a parachute drop, a sailboat race, a flagpole sitting, an air show, or a skate-in for charity. (Whether your dignity is simultaneously compromised while sitting atop a flagpole is entirely your call.) Each of these events has a high visual factor, and television news programs rely on visual stories to break the monotony of talking heads. (Likewise newspapers and magazines appreciate good pictures as well as text.) That's why fires get such extraordinary play on television, although I hesitate to suggest that you burn your dwellings to the ground for purposes of publicity (at least without consulting your insurance agent in advance). Even when the building in question is a deserted, collapsing warehouse in some remote locale, if a camera crew can get there while the flames are towering it's a shoo-in for the six o'clock news.

So if the story you want to tell has a visual aspect, start with the news department of a television station. The event doesn't have to be as spectacular and colorful as a balloon race. Let's say your local schoolhouse is in desperate need of tuck-pointing (so desperate that a child can pull a brick loose by hand). This fact is likely to escape the attention of a network program like *Meet the Press*, but local stations should be enticed. You are on a committee trying to get a badly needed school bond issue passed in the face of a tax rebellion by the electorate. School bonds and rebellious taxpayers are not very sexy, but the sight of an eight-year-old prying a brick from a structurally unsafe building makes a dramatic point and, in exchange, the local reporter will allow you a few words on camera to explain how the bond issue would make this building safe for helpless, innocent children. You get what you want; the press gets what it wants.

Armed with that triumph, you can call the producer of a local talk show and probably sell him or her on a slot to talk about how unsafe the buildings are. Once there you also can pitch your bond issue.

Sometimes the cause you are peddling is merely a smokescreen for something else. Let's say you're a lawyer with political ambitions in the local mayoralty race two years from now. Your name is not exactly a household word, and attempting to get air time under your true colors is fruitless. But there is nothing to stop you from taking up the cudgel for some issue around which you intend to base your forthcoming campaign. You can form a citizens' committee for honesty in government, or a citizens' committee to construct a stadium, or a citizens' committee to preserve Mulberry Gardens. Find a dramatic way to expostulate, and you're flying.

This is not to suggest that everyone who forms a citizens' committee has ulterior motives (although it's been known to happen). It illustrates how a very personal goal of becoming mayor can be transformed into an issue that affects a great many people.

By and large when you want to use the power of television and the press to communicate, you must exhibit and demonstrate that your cause is of interest or benefit to the public at large. But a worthy cause is not enough in itself. You must have something new to say about the subject, something you have discovered yourself, contrived yourself, or dramatized in a newsworthy fashion. Tradition or civic spirit may get you a berth on that local talk show without a tidbit of real news, but it won't command and sustain the audience's attention, and that's what you're really after.

This becomes particularly hard when your cause is an annual event. One woman, faced with promoting an auction to benefit the orchestra in a small city, found herself with none of the sale items at hand as she pitched herself to a television talk show. Instead, she did her homework on the diminishing funding available to arts organizations across the country, and was able to plead the cause of the auction with considerable eloquence.

Ultimately the importance of your cause is less important than the style in which you sell it. (Sizzle counts for more than steak, particularly on television.) If you are an original personality, you may not need a forceful tailwind to land a talk show berth. But if you aren't, there are ways to sell your cause anyhow, sometimes even when there is no news.

1. Is there a way to demonstrate a perceived benefit to many people from your cause? (The benefit need only be perceived, not real.)
2. Is there a way to package your cause that makes it seem new, even if it's old? (A more recent set of statistics can do the job.)
3. Is there a dramatic way to illustrate your cause, even if your message is decades old? (Charts, films, slides, tapes, and testimonials.)
4. Can you demonstrate a particular expertise in talking about a subject of continuing public interest? (A favorite ploy of physicians, lawyers, and other professionals who are somewhat constrained in advertising widely, but who use broadcast exposure as a way to build a practice.)

Why go to all that trouble? Because you want to communicate with a great many people. It doesn't matter if your motive is selfish; what matters is that you want to reach as large an audience as possible.

If that is your goal television and the press are your means. And the only way to succeed is by talking in public to reporters and answering their questions.

How to Get on the Air

There's always the simplest procedure: you call the host on the phone and ask if you can be on the show. If the host won't talk to you, speak to a producer. They're sometimes called *bookers*. Most programs are booked by someone other than the star, and the bigger the show the more bookers there are. (I should add that your performance on a program begins with that phone call, because broadcasters are schooled to preinterview prospective guests to determine their air-worthiness. That phone call is the first plateau, so be alive!) If the show prefers its requests from guests in writing, keep it to one page of typing with just a few clippings attached to help support your point and credibility. Follow up with another phone call a few days afterwards. Don't call later than an hour before the show goes on the air. After that point, the host and staff will be too busy to talk. And immediately after a show the host is as wrung out as you will be after your bravura performance, and definitely not in the mood to hear about the school bond issue.

Simple as this procedure is, it also has its pitfalls, so do your homework first. In any given market there may be 2 to 20 alternatives to choose from, some of them programs with definite subject limitations. For example, it would not be the wisest course to argue the cause of community theater on the 5 A.M. farm hour. But it might work nicely on a local issues talk show on your educational TV station. Sell yourself in the slots that look most logical. That may mean combing your local TV listings to cull the talk shows on the schedule. Then watch them beforehand. Don't let 2 A.M. time slots bother you as many of those programs are taped at a more civilized hour. Do the same with the radio stations. If your local newspaper doesn't print full radio schedules you may have to do some listening around the dial to find your mark. It's worth the effort.

In your peregrinations around the channel selector and across the AM and FM radio dials, try not to let the commercials be your guide. The host isn't responsible for what the sales department hath wrought, and many stations require advertisers to buy their spots around the clock. This means that a sponsor's six commercials per day may run on a rotating basis in a 24 hour period, but not always in time slots of the advertiser's or host's choosing.

If you are going to do one of those 2 A.M. talk shows on television, and the ads are all for TV offerings of someone's greatest hits or newfangled kitchen gadgets, you can assume that commercial rates at this hour are somewhat lower than usual, and that the audience at home is equivalently smaller. This should not deter you in a choice of debut, but you should be aware that a berth on such a show will not get your message across to the multitudes. It is, however, a good place to practice before you take your act on the road to the higher rated shows in better time slots.

(This, too, is a matter of perspective. It is perfectly true that not all programs on which you may appear will be seen by the masses. Sometimes the audience will be 20,000, not 5,000,000. But 20,000 people is a full house at Madison Square Garden.)

When you've found a likely show, watch or listen to it a few times before you call. Familiarity can breed respect and admiration from the host.

If you have a PR representative like the late Ivy Lee, you don't have to bother with this rigmarole, and it's easier, as long as he or she approaches the project in the same spirit. My buddy, Barry Farber (a television and radio talk show host in New York City), once wrote the following guidelines, "How NOT to Get on the Barry Farber Show," in hopes of educating the public relations fraternity:

1. When calling to pitch one of your clients for an interview, do not begin by asking, "Are you still on the air?"
2. If for some reason you insist on that opening above all others, at least don't sound so incredulous when we reply in the affirmative.
3. I will (according to which is most appropriate) congratulate, kiss, or marry the first PR person who says: "Look, a great

talker my client isn't, but he's got a lot of important information that a lesser interviewer than you couldn't possibly elicit."

4. Don't ask: "How long is he going to be on?" It's like lovemaking. We'll both know 10 seconds before it's over.

5. Having promised me a great guest who will strike down my competitors with terminal envy, and who thereupon starts out weak and gradually tapers off, do not (while I am applying mouth-to-mouth resuscitation, feeling for his pulse, and signaling the engineer to hurry in with his harmonica) tell me about another of your clients who's even better!

On that note, Barry concludes his treatise as follows: "In dealing with us, bear in mind: honesty is always one of the alternatives."

Farber speaks for more than himself. Be honest about why you want to be on the show, what you have to offer, and what you cannot supply. If none of these strikes the host's fancy, ask why. There may be a good reason, or you may just have struck out. If the host explains, listen carefully. If he or she has no reason, ask if you can rethink it and call or write again. Do not, however, ask the host to recommend another show or approach for you. It's not his business to act as your counsel, and making that request is a professional insult, leaving the impression that his program didn't matter that much anyway if another one is more likely to accept you.

Another sure-fire way to get yourself on local television and radio is through a friend or connection (maybe a big advertiser) at the station in question. If getting on a program means more to you than life itself, ask the sponsor to put pressure on the host through the sales department. The star will be annoyed but, if you are positive you can handle the situation, go ahead and pull your strings.

Garnering a second invitation to appear on the same program is truly the acid test of your excellence on the air, and it will be forthcoming from the staff if you were dazzling the first time around. There is no other way. At another of my alma mater stations in Chicago, WGN, Jim Loughman held forth on a talk show for more than a decade. "If I were to give advice to potential guests on television or radio shows, it would be this," he told me. "*Dare to be different*. If you have something to say, find a way to make it interesting. Don't approach things in a given way just because you've always seen it done that way on *Donahue* or *Meet the Press*. Do your homework. Think things through. And then find a way to express your thoughts in a manner that is meaningful *and* innovative. If you can get *my* attention, chances are I'll hear you. If not, chances are I'll assume that I already have—at least a hundred times!"

I asked for Jim's opinion as a veteran host about the best guests: "Basically, I wanted interesting people with strongly held views," he said. "All the better if they were newsmakers. A smart PR man or woman could unearth that much in a 10-second conversation with my secretary. I was open to any pitch from any person that was seemingly honest, straightforward, and compatible with my program format.

"The best guests I interviewed were not necessarily ultra-high-profile. It gets back to what I mentioned a moment ago about strongly held views. The other side of the coin is the willingness, even eagerness, to express and defend those views; to mix it up with friends and foes alike; to be stimulating and provocative."

I also wanted to know about the worst guests: "They were the ones who acted like all they had to do was show up; people who rested on their press clippings, or put on airs, or spoke condescendingly to the audience. Politicians come to mind. Lots of them."

As a guest on any program, it is helpful to know beforehand how long you are expected to appear, so you can plan your remarks and presentation accordingly. But as Barry Farber implies, that's partly up to you; it can be a variable factor, not always fixed in advance.

Jim Loughman agrees: "Any seasoned program host can tell within five minutes after the red light goes on whether the guest is a keeper. If he starts out dull and rapidly regresses, the host has no choice, brutal as it may seem. You show him the door—politely and charitably if possible, but unceremoniously if necessary. That's easy if he's joining you by telephone; not so easy if he's sitting two feet away. Still, your first responsibility is to yourself—if you want to keep your job—and to your audience, which expects a certain level of competence. In the words of one of my favorite philosophers, Red Auerbach: 'Show me a good loser, and I'll show you a loser!'

"When first-time guests appeared on my program, or persons I knew had no broadcast experience, I made a special effort to put them at ease. I urged them to relax and imagine that we were sitting in a booth at a restaurant or bar, or at home in their living room, just having a conversation. If they were dressed to the teeth"—this is radio, remember—"I urged the men to loosen their ties and remove their jackets, if they wished. If the women were wearing earrings, I mentioned that they might be more comfortable without them, since they would have to wear earphones" (for the call-in portions of the program).

"There was one other standing rule on my program. I always told guests in advance that I would leave time in the program to let them mention anything that was important to them that I might have missed. I guess that came about early in my career when I got tired of hearing people say: 'Gee, I wish we'd had time to mention. . . .' I figured, what the hell, if they were willing to take the time to participate in the show, the least I could do was let them have their say. Of course, I always retained the right to question them closely about anything and everything they brought up.

"I'm not sure I ever *helped* a guest on the air, other than extending the basic courtesies which I've just described. There were times when I saw a guest struggling to come up with the right word or phrase and, if I suspected I knew what it was, I offered it.

"On the other hand, I felt no remorse at turning full force on pompous asses, pseudo-intellectuals, bigots of all stripes, and almost anyone who enriched himself at the public trough. This may sound holier-than-thou, and I really don't mean it that way, but there were times when I really got pissed-off by things people would say and do."

In the beginning of this book, Robert MacNeil made a reference to talk show hosts who "generally play God." But down deep, both MacNeil and I are on Jim Loughman's side.

By the time any broadcaster or reporter gets a measure of reputation, he or she has seen more pretension, and has been told more lies, than an IRS agent. Sometimes they are bold, black lies, sometimes subtle half-truths:

> The Schmidlap Widget Company cordially invites you to meet the president of SWC at 10 A.M. Monday in the executive offices of the company where he will make a major announcement of far-reaching significance about a new research development that will have a vast impact on automobile gas mileage.

Taking no chances, all three commercial networks, the wire services, 14 major newspapers, 3 news magazines, and all the local stations and papers in a 100-mile radius show up at Schmidlap headquarters, ready to transmit this great and momentous announcement to an eager and deserving public. At the appointed hour the president of the Widget Company unveils a new device that car buyers can purchase as an option on next year's models: a microprocessor-run display gizmo, telling exactly how gas mileage varies at different speeds and driving conditions. You don't get more miles per gallon, you simply know how many, or few, you're getting.

Politicians are probably the best at this ploy. Every candidate in every presidential campaign has a major announcement to make at every airport landing. Usually the announcement is merely a vaguely worded rehash of the story already appearing in the morning papers, followed by five minutes of gushing about how thrilled he is to be in (he turns to his press secretary for a hurried conversation) "the great city of Springfield" (he finishes triumphantly).

Couple incessant repetitions of those experiences with silly evasions and gross overstatements by PR agents, business moguls, authors, and the remaining potpourri of available people, and you can understand a reporter's cynicism and impatience. Any interviewer who hears a writer say, "I demonstrate conclusively in my book that hypnotism should replace psychiatry," has some reason for skepticism or annoyance.

That is why Jim Loughman and others like him occasionally are irritated by things people say and do, and thank heaven they sometimes play God.

Earlier in this chapter I referred (for at least the second time around) to the standard H-and-W questions, and I also made the point that an interviewer, particularly a talk show host, is likely to explore other areas of inquiry, too. As Robert MacNeil has written: "He is not even required to ask questions a journalist would consider *relevant*."

Please turn the page. You are about to be inoculated against the perils of an irrelevant question, and four additional types of questions that interviewers on television and elsewhere are apt to pose.

chapter seven
The Irrelevant Question

An *irrelevancy* is anything that has "no application or effect in a specified circumstance." For the most part, press interviews are focused on particular topics or themes—but not always, and not entirely.

They also may spill into other areas of conversation, which may be related and even unrelated to the matter at hand. A reporter may be legitimately curious about other facets of your life or career, and interested in your opinions and comments on diverse subjects wholly unconnected with the recent emission at your chemical plant. It may be your unfortunate indictment and conviction 15 years ago for an illegal contribution of $10,000 to CREEP, or the succession plan within your company upon your demise (perhaps sooner than you expect).

On radio and television, if you've come to promote a new product the plug can be accomplished in two minutes or less. Eight minutes, or an hour, of air time may remain, which can open Pandora's box.

How widely it's opened should be a matter of considerable attention, not that you have anything in particular to conceal, but because your comments can be misconstrued in a freewheeling conversation. And in broadcasting, the conversations are apt to be exactly that: freewheeling.

For instance, an inexpensive and lazy format on radio is to invite the audience to participate by telephone, which accounts for the proliferation and frequency of call-in shows in America, where listeners do part of the work. (The callers don't receive payment for their contributions to the proceedings, and the phone company bills them at the end of the month, not the radio station.) In the main, sane people listen to such programs. But disproportionately, it's the screwballs and exhibitionists who call in. The latter are lonely, frustrated, or drunk; they're demented; some are extremists; and so on. You are apt to be asked anything of a relevant or irrelevant nature, and are likely to be chastised, especially at night. (The urgency of your cause notwithstanding, it is best to decline such appearances during a full moon phase.)

On a TV talk show, you may be joined by other guests, thrown together as a panel without any thought to what you may have in common. On my last visit to *The Joe Franklin Show* in New York City, I shared the overstuffed sofa with Joan Fontaine (the actress), Dong Kingman (the commercial artist), and an Italian balladeer whose name I don't recall (opening that very night at a supper club in Queens). Years ago in Chicago, another talk show host began his program with approximately these words, "Tonight we'll talk about energy policy with John Cardinal Cody and the fabulous Gabor sisters."

So there you sit next to a comedian, a vegetarian, a flyweight boxer, a skydiver, and a microbiologist. When such a motley bunch starts talking about the impact of a recent Supreme Court decision, a guest who is seriously affected by the discussion can be compromised. An offhand statement, along with the speaker's affiliation and title, might be taken out of context and played on the nightly news.

That brings me to a first reminder, which seems on the surface too obvious to belabor, but often is neglected. Unless your name is Frank Sinatra or Henry Kissinger, most people in the audience won't remember it when the program is over. They will remember your affiliation, however, and maybe your title.

Therefore it follows that anything you say will be attributed, not necessarily to you by name, but to the enterprise or organization that you represent. No disclaimer, such as "speaking strictly for myself . . . ," is likely to change that fact; at least for those 10 minutes on a talk show, insofar as the audience is concerned, you are Chevrolet (despite the fact that you merely work as a mechanic for a car dealership in Portland, Maine).

Any topic is likely to be fair game once an interview commences. But when it's over, the audience will remember that a man or woman "from Bristol-Myers" was talking about analgesics, tax reform and Supreme Court decisions about commercial speech.

Here is a horrible example (which actually occurred, but I've changed the names to protect the victim). On just such a TV talk show (with the flyweight fighter, the stand-up comic, and assorted others), the subject of marijuana came up, which is a subject on which everyone has an opinion, however ill-informed. In the midst of this freewheeling discussion, it was time to introduce yet another face on the program, simultaneously bidding farewell to the aging matinee idol who had to scamper to his dinner theater performance (all duly plugged by title, location, and length of run).

HOST: Our next guest is Mr. Wonderful, president of Youth Services of America. Mr. Wonderful is also a practicing attorney in Duluth, Minnesota. As a lawyer, sir, do you think marijuana should be legalized?

MR. WONDERFUL: Well, speaking just for myself, I have long felt that the marijuana laws are too harsh.

HOST: Then you do believe it should be legalized?

MR. WONDERFUL: Certainly decriminalized, yes.

Then it was the vegetarian's turn to discuss marijuana's herbal properties, and the microbiologist's turn to discuss the dangers of paraquat contamination.

Harmless drivel, right? And before the show was over, each panelist got a moment to plug his or her special project. Mr. Wonderful, in fact, lived up to his name with an impassioned plea on behalf of inner city groups, and a beautifully recited anecdote about a gang leader who persuaded his flock to affiliate with Youth Services and how this led to college scholarships for many of them and good jobs for those whose formal educations stopped after high school.

But the next day in the newspapers, and on television too, the president of Youth Services came off a little differently. "Youth Services Chief Says Marijuana Not a Crime" was the newspaper headline. And guess what segment from the talk show made the evening news on TV?

MR. WONDERFUL: I have long felt that the marijuana laws are too harsh.

HOST: Then you do believe it should be legalized?

MR. WONDERFUL: Certainly decriminalized, yes.

You can discuss anything you choose with the press and on television, as long as you remember that you are quotable, and that you will not necessarily be quoted in context. The newspaper readers and TV viewers who hadn't seen the talk show didn't know or care that Mr. Wonderful, also an officer of the court in Duluth, was merely participating in an ongoing conversation to exhaust the remaining air time. They didn't hear or care how the host started his question, which was "as a lawyer, sir. . . ." And no amount of "speaking just for myself" or "in my personal opinion" disassociated or distanced the answer from the speaker's affiliation: "Youth Services Chief Says. . . ."

This danger is particularly great on a talk show that is prerecorded for later broadcast. Often these programs are not shown in the most advantageous time periods, and one way they can entice audiences is with teaser promotional spots. What better come-on could there be than that little snippet of Mr. Wonderful from Youth Services more or less endorsing marijuana?

Television is a business, remember, and audiences are the customers.

On TV a person's title is further established and implanted graphically, and is sometimes even conferred. On the lower-third of the screen, across Mr. Wonderful's shirt front, a two-line superimposition (called a *lower-third* in television parlance) is likely to appear:

President
Youth Services of America

In my most recent stint as an oracle for CBS, I was awarded five different lower-third titles during America's 50TH presidential campaign (and I was asked for my permission about *none* of them in advance).

On my first appearance on Channel 2 in New York I was strictly a "Media Consultant." Next I was promoted (or otherwise) to "Political Consultant," then to "Political Commentator," later to "Political Analyst," and finally to the pinnacle, which was "Political Expert."

After my recitations on the five o'clock news, I occasionally repaired to a saloon in close proximity to the CBS Broadcast Center on West 57TH Street in Manhattan, where sometimes I would overhear my remarks strenuously rehashed by local patrons who had watched the program. But never that I can recall was a comment or opinion attributed to me by name. It was always attributed to CBS, or to that amorphous expert whose countenance and image had flickered on the establishment's TV screen 30 minutes previously.

Relating those experiences to Mr. Wonderful, what should he have done instead as he sat there on television with "Youth Services" plastered across his torso?

First, he should have remembered why he was there, which was not as a Duluth lawyer, a charming fellow, or an original thinker, but because of his avocational involvements with disadvantaged youngsters. In that role, he should have remembered that certain subjects are off-limits, dangerous, and, in fact, subjects about which a person with his title can say little or nothing—safely.

If he had a finely tuned sense of humor, Mr. Wonderful could have grinned at the question and defused it:

(Sincere chuckle) You're asking the president of Youth Services if I think *marijuana* should be *legalized!*

(Then more soberly) When the matter of controlled substances comes up for discussion at the clubhouse, we're more likely to be talking about *abuse*, not availability.

Or:

Fundamentally what we preach, and I hope successfully *teach* at Youth Services, is respect for the laws. It's not our function to make them, only obey them, whether we always agree. Besides (bridge) we have a more pressing issue to work on... (and he is off to the races with his story about saving troubled kids).

It helps in such situations to think of yourself as the personification of your title and affiliation. What might be an issue of great interest and firm feeling to you, the person, may not be an issue on which someone of your title should comment. Before you answer an irrelevant question, think how it will look attributed to your organization tomorrow in the papers or tonight on the TV news.

That leads to my second reminder: matters of relevancy and irrelevancy are shared decisions between you and an interviewer. You are not a puppy on a leash to be jerked hither and yon against your will from topic to topic. You can (should, must) participate in the conversational deciding.

It's useful to fix a definition of *relevant* in your head at the outset. Mine is the following: if it's extraneous in my representative capacity, it is irrelevant, and usually I'll dodge it (I hope gracefully and graciously). If it's extraneous to my purpose in the interview, ditto. If it's dangerous, I will avoid it like bubonic plague (even gracelessly).

But not all irrelevancies are potentially harmful. Some are merely, well, irrelevant, or frothy. Don't be too rigid. Good advice is like suntan lotion. Use enough of it, but not too much or too little.

If Mr. Wonderful had been queried during the same interview about his previous career in the National Basketball Association, I might have suggested a short period of accommodation and answering, not stonewalling. However, the emphasis is on the word short. Every minute devoted to slam dunking is a minute not devoted to Youth Services.

The watchwords here are control and rationing: the time apportioned by you for frivolous chatter should be limited, hopefully expanding the time devoted to your principal cause.

chapter eight
Let's Pretend

In the lore of American politics, it was Franklin Delano Roosevelt who first labeled them for what they are: "iffy questions." That was at least 50 years ago, and unless it suited his purpose, which rarely occurred, President Roosevelt steadfastly refused to answer them on grounds of their iffiness alone.

The asking of those questions hasn't stopped, however. Among the multitude of Democratic candidates for the presidential nomination in 1984, Gary Hart was the most seriously impaled when he agreed to play let's pretend on national television. It happened in Atlanta on PBS two nights before the Georgia primary. His playmate was John Chancellor of *NBC News*.

Chancellor wanted to know the following: as president, what would Hart do if he was awakened in the dead of night and informed by the White House staff that a Czechoslovakian airliner had strayed off course and was cruising over Nebraska? Would he shoot it down, or what?

Accepting a bizarre hypothesis is generally the first step to catastrophe with an iffy question. Dismissing it or altering it to suit is recommended instead.

Could a Czechoslovakian airliner remain undetected until it reached Nebraska? It's almost impossible to conjure with a straight face, but Mr. Hart pulled it off that night in Atlanta.

Not wanting to appear warlike, the Senator allowed that he would dispatch Air Force planes with instructions for the pilots to

peer in the windows of the airliner to determine if the Czechoslo-
vakians aboard were in uniform! (Unexplained by Hart at the time was
how such a feat could be accomplished at supersonic speeds, although
Senator Glenn, the former astronaut, couldn't wait to bring it up
afterwards.)

A few weeks previously in New Hampshire, the game was
played somewhat differently with the Democratic candidates by Ted
Koppel and Phil Donahue on another TV debate. Hypothetical
questions were posed (of course), but the participants were told about
them in advance, which tends to mitigate the chances for a world-
class gaffe.

At the time I said in one of my CBS commentaries:

I think the liveliest parts of Sunday's debate were the hypothetical
or "iffy" questions, which the candidates were given 45 seconds to
answer—questions like, "What would you do *if* Iran blocked the
Straits?" and "What *if* another of our embassies is seized
somewhere?"

They make for great television, but they're not representative of how
a president functions in office, because world crises don't develop in
an instant, needing to be solved in the next instant.

Getting an "iffy" question is like having a bomb rolled under your
chair with the fuse lit.

Usually we advise politicians to politely decline them at news
conferences because of their speculative nature.

The difference last night was the candidates were alerted about
them in advance, so they had some time beforehand to compose
their answers.

Anticipating or knowing the questions in advance makes it
easy, if you accept my admonishment a few chapters ago about
extemporaneous speech. Time to compose a response, and be
composed in answering, removes much of the danger. But you'll
rarely, if ever, be afforded such time in an interview. More likely,
without warning a similar bomb will be rolled in your direction; it
frequently happens to politicians.

A typical exchange on television begins as follows: "I know you haven't announced your candidacy, but what if Governor Incumbent makes good on his implication not to run for reelection?"

Thanks to FDR, even the greenest politico has learned to reply: "Until the governor makes a definitive statement, it's premature for me to speculate on what I might or might not do." Then, if the guest has been doing his homework, he bridges deftly to the topic he prefers, as follows: "Really, Fred, I don't think people are interested in useless speculation, particularly when they've just had a dose of the new seven percent sales tax. You know I've been deeply involved in the effort to streamline our state's tax structure—an effort to reduce the burden on the individual taxpayer...."

Most politicians have been trained to sniff a hypothetical question a mile away, but other talk show participants, lamentably, can be seduced into playing the game. The trick is to keep your sonar tuned when the questioning changes from straightforward to conditional. If you don't decline or demur, the following is an excruciating example (gleaned from one of my practice sessions with an oil man) of what might happen.

First the tortuous question:

HOST: In one of Paul Erdman's books, he presents a very convincing scenario for nuclear war in the Middle East. Considering the revolution in Iran and Mr. Erdman's rather startling predictions about the area, do you think, *if* the United States were faced with an anti-American coup in Saudi Arabia, that something similar might happen? This is not to suggest that yours or any other oil company would be part of such a plan. But *if* the situation were to explode in Saudi Arabia as it did in Iran, do you think the U.S. might just go in and secure those oil fields before something happened to them? Of course I'm not suggesting in any way that you would have anything to do with an actual U.S. invasion of Saudi Arabia, but do you think it could happen?

Forget the abundant disclaimers. Forget the mitigating phrases that seem to disassociate the executive from the burden of aggression. Even though Mr. Oil thanked the reporter for his care in framing that question, he went right ahead and answered it by outlining a detailed plan of attack on Saudi Arabia to make its oil fields safe for American consumers. By the time he got through, nobody in the audience remembered the disclaimer, only this horrifying, meticulous plan to invade someone else's country.

In each of these examples, I have flagged the word *if* in italics. But iffy questions also come in various disguises, many omitting the word *if,* such as: "Mr. Mondale, let's say...," and "Senator Hart, let's suppose...."

Both are iffy questions already, but without an *if* anywhere in sight.

Even more diabolical are the following examples:

"Fighting it right now at present strength, who would win a conventional war between the U.S. and the Soviet Union?"

"Could the Green Bay Packers of the late 60s defeat last year's Super Bowl champions?"

Again, no *ifs* appear in those decidedly iffy questions, although you may choose to answer either one, the iffiness notwithstanding. That's the point: it's your choice. A press interview, if you keep your wits about you, shouldn't resemble a stampede of spooked mustangs. Answer voluntarily if you wish; never answer involuntarily. And if you choose to decline, your excuse is inherent in the framework of the question itself: its nature is speculative or conditional (which, if you choose, you can label wildly speculative, and substitute something more tame).

Bear with me as I demonstrate another example of an if-less iffy question (the most insidious I devised during the 1984 presidential campaign). I was speculating in a broadcast commentary after the New Hampshire primary about how Phil Donahue might have handled the Lincoln–Douglas debates, had there been television in 1858:

I can see him now admist an outdoor audience, the two candidates in a blaze of light on a wooden platform with a railing in front.

Their prepared remarks having been delivered, Phil now looks quizzically at the towering Mr. Lincoln and the portly Mr. Douglas, and asks:

"You'd like your sister to marry a slave. Yes or no?"

Anyone who can answer that question without disquieting or enflaming a substantial portion of the U.S. populace shouldn't be wasting his or her time reading this book.

chapter nine
The Inconsistency Trap

Starting a chapter with a citation from the late Saul Alinsky's *Rules for Radicals* is risking alienation of affections charges from everyone whose politics are to the right of Mark Green's. (I haven't commissioned a poll, but that might include 80 percent of the American people.)

Nevertheless (for those few of you still reading) Mr. Alinsky, recalling Abraham Lincoln, reports a classic example of what I call *the inconsistency trap*, a trap into which (and needlessly) many press interviewees have fallen.

Alinsky wrote, "This was also the same Lincoln who, a few years prior to his signing the Emancipation Proclamation, stated in his first inaugural address: 'I do but quote from one of (my) speeches when I declared that I have no purpose, directly or indirectly, to interfere with the institution of slavery in the States where it exists. I believe I have no lawful right to do so, and I have no inclination to do so. Those who nominated and elected me did so with full knowledge that I made this and many similar declarations, and have never recanted them.'"

To which Alinsky added, "Those who would be critical of the ethics of Lincoln's reversal of positions have a strangely unreal picture of a static, unchanging world, where one remains firm and committed to certain so-called principles or positions. In the politics of human life, consistency is *not* a virtue. To be consistent means, according to the Oxford University Dictionary, 'standing still or not moving.' Men must change with the times or die."

Those words likely were written by Mr. Alinsky from the deepest recesses of a jailhouse, places in which he occasionally found himself incarcerated for provoking or advocating change at a faster pace than the remainder of society was willing to permit and accept. But that doesn't obviate the wisdom of his conviction: "Men must change with the times or die." Neither you nor your ideas are necessarily embedded in concrete or the past, except at your own insistence. Times and circumstances change. Opinions and commitments can change, too, without loss of face. (His life may have been tormented and difficult, but President Lincoln was never confronted by Sam Donaldson, who would have asked him about that contradiction repeatedly.)

Remember that place we formerly called Red China? It was barbaric and dark, especially in the view of Richard Nixon. Later in Nixon's career, Mao Tse-tung and Chou En-lai became two of his favorite supper partners.

And that inconsistency is hardly unprecedented in the annals of world alignments. In World War II, the United States was allied with the Soviet Union against Germany, Japan, and Italy. Shortly thereafter we switched sides. If nations can change their stances with impunity, why can't the rest of us?

It can happen, without warning, to any guest on any television or radio show. Suddenly the interviewer says: "In 1980, you were saying such and such. Now you're saying something sharply contradictory. Why is that?"

If the question is entirely unexpected, it can throw a guest over the edge of panic. His or her face flushes, perhaps even visibly through the pancake. The pulse races, that awful metallic taste rises on the back of the tongue, and the front of the tongue starts tripping over lame excuses: "Well, look...it really isn't all that, uh, contradictory. What happened was that...well, this happened, and that happened, you know. And in light of whereas, wherefore and whereby, you can see now...."

The guest has fallen into the trap. He has been accused of being inconsistent, or worse, opportunistic, and his reaction has done nothing to allay the suspicions suddenly raised in the minds of the audience.

Who said that your views have been irrevocably transcribed into the permanent record after a first public utterance? When faced with a charge of inconsistency, admit it. You are allowed to change your mind. In fact, it shows growth and flexibility. If you once felt that way but no longer do, just say so: "Yes, it's true I made that statement in 1980. But I've changed my mind," or, "When I said that, my firsthand investigation of the situation wasn't complete. I've subsequently finished it, and it's made a difference in my opinion."

My favorite example of a reversal with audacity and good humor was Ronald Reagan's in the 1980 TV debate with President Carter. Formerly an ardent fan of Franklin Roosevelt, the Republican candidate was called to account for his declarations of praise for the policies of FDR. "(When I made those comments in the 30s and 40s) I *was* a Democrat," Mr. Reagan responded. "I said a lot of dumb things in those days."

It's not a sin to change your mind for good reasons. It's also not a good idea to change your mind on weighty matters too often. If you do, people might conclude that you shoot off your mouth without sufficient forethought; they may perceive you as wishy-washy, undependable, or a loose cannon. One 180-degree turn per serious issue per lifetime is approximately the limit.

The sum total of a person's opinions on the issues of his time is what makes that person identifiable. Thus, if you are compelled to change your mind about an important issue, don't dismiss it too airily. Take the time, as President Reagan did subsequently, to explain why your opinion was modified. The worst thing you can do in a broadcast situation is to leave an audience with the impression that your old view still prevails. If they agree with your old view, they will be very upset to find out later that you no longer hold it. And if they disagree with your previous position, it's important for you to make it perfectly clear that you have come around to their way of thinking.

Only a favored few (like Mr. Reagan) can get away with flippancy. A beloved character (the late Sam Ervin), a certified curmudgeon (Barry Goldwater), perhaps, can say: "My head bone wasn't connected to my tongue," or words to that effect. It may work for them, but unless you are similarly beloved or certified, don't emulate that tactic in public for any serious issue.

For some reason, people who can be perfectly frank about many embarrassing topics have a hard time admitting "I've changed my mind." They find it even harder to say "I was wrong."

In 1948, South Carolina's Strom Thurmond ran for president of the United States on the Dixiecrat ticket. During his campaign, he said, "There aren't enough troops in the army to force southern people to admit negroes into our theaters, swimming pools, and homes." Thirty years later in 1978, Thurmond delivered a Senate speech in support of a bill to make the District of Columbia a state. Its two senators and one representative would, no doubt, be black. Thurmond said, "I think it's the fair thing to do." Shall we conclude that Mr. Thurmond favored the admittance of more blacks to Congress, but not to swimming pools and theaters in South Carolina?

When you change your mind about an important issue on which you've taken a strong stand in the past, you should say so publicly and without equivocation. Whether it's a simple matter of new evidence or a radical change of heart, you must explain. Otherwise you'll bite your tongue talking out of both sides of your mouth.

As previously related, one of the most memorable pratfalls in broadcasting history was taken by George Romney in 1968 on the late Lou Gordon's radio program in Detroit.

GORDON: Governor, you used to be a hawk on Vietnam, but now you're a dove. What happened?

ROMNEY: I was brainwashed.

Romney should have given the explanation of his reversal the time it deserved. He might have said: "You know, Lou, I've been insecure with my position about this controversial war. I wasn't sure of it. So I went over there for a couple of weeks to see for myself—at my own expense, incidentally. I tromped around in the jungles and had conversations with a lot of people who really know what's going on. And their comments and opinions didn't jibe with what the Joint Chiefs had told us. The bottom-line is that I changed my mind, and now I'm convinced that I'm right."

Paranoically, however, some government figures are gun-shy about true confessions and prefer to obfuscate. One of them was W. Michael Blumenthal, ill-fated Treasury Secretary for two years under Jimmy Carter, and previously the chief executive officer at Bendix Corporation. Using syntax that may remind you of Casey Stengel, Mr. Blumenthal once said:

> Another example of how significant it is how you appear to the press—and how different that is in government as compared to in a corporation—has to do with the risk of changing your mind. A businessman is entitled and expected to change his mind, and there's no particular opprobrium attached to that at all. You get new facts, conditions change, the markets change, industries change, you get a new contract or you lose one, you talk to more people. You say, all right, let's abort it. Let's slow it down, or let's do something else. What counts in the end is how you come out, not whether you've changed your mind or not.
>
> In the government, if you change your mind, you're accused of inconsistency.
>
> That's one reason there's a lot of double-talk in Washington. I found that politicians and secretaries of the Treasury have to go to great lengths to avoid appearing to have changed their minds, or to rationalize the fact that they're changing their minds, or to leave enough leeway in their statements so that the press never knows that they're changing their minds. Otherwise they get a finger pointed at them.

Mr. Blumenthal concluded his statement with good advice on other topics—to counterbalance the aforementioned. He said:

> When you come into the (Treasury) job, you learn, often by mistakes, that there are code words you must avoid, and others you can use to state a certain proposition.

You don't speculate about hypothetical alternatives (see the last chapter) and you don't allow newsmen to draw you into choices between two *unacceptable* alternatives (see the next one).

chapter ten
Bottom Line Cohen

Actually, his first name was Alan, at least until he took charge of the hapless New York Rangers of the National Hockey League in the mid-1970s. A tax lawyer, Mr. Cohen was nevertheless unable to arrest that club's stagnant financial condition, reported *The New York Times*.

"In fact," said the *Times*, "Cohen came to be considered part of the problem, an impression rooted in his response to a question a reporter posed early in his tenure. Would Cohen, the newsman wondered, rather have a Stanley Cup (for the Rangers) or a profit?"

He gave his answer: "a profit," and thereafter was known for the remainder of his term as Bottom Line Cohen.

It's an example of what I call *the A or B dilemma*. It occurs frequently, probably stemming from the human love of simplicity rather than from actual malice.

In broadcast news especially, interviewers and tape editors seek short, no-nonsense replies, sparing audiences long, complicated explanations. They want to keep their programs moving at a brisk pace.

"Is your company more interested in profits, or the public welfare?"

"Which country is nuttier to deal with—Syria or Libya?"

The A or B dilemma is a favorite ploy of talk show hosts and TV newsmen. At its worst, it causes obfuscation of the issues and confuses communication instead of enhancing it. At its best, it's not a particularly thought-provoking way to delve into an issue.

Why, then, does it occur so often? Is it just laziness or incompetence on the reporter's part?

Usually it is neither. Whether a filmed or taped interview is two minutes or two hours long, it must contain excerptible material to justify the expenditure. In the interview itself, a reporter won't constrain a subject to responses of 15 seconds or less, although such a snippet may be all that is destined for broadcast. Instead, the reporter may construct questions that will, by themselves, elicit brief, pithy answers. A news broadcast cannot cover all the ramifications of a topic. TV wants answers that are short and simple. And most times, because so few people are initiated into the vagaries of the broadcast interview, the A or B dilemma question gets short, simple, extractable responses even when the questions are ridiculous.

When a person who is expected to answer such impossible questions actually tries to do so, the level of the program as a medium of information drops precipitously. It does so not only because the answer is usually as inane as the question, but because the interviewee has surrendered his autonomy. From there on, the reporter or host becomes the authority figure. He has proved to be the manipulator. If you, the guest, lose control of a question, you lose control of the interview. And if the host has a particular dislike for you or your cause, it's an entree to squash you like a grape underfoot.

It's one thing to know what the fundamentals are and another to use them properly. All the conviction, preparation, and determination you can possibly muster for a given situation will do no good if you suffer an attack of blind panic, or worse, surrender your independence to the host.

The broadcast studio is a foreign land for many talk show guests, but its similarities to real life are greater than its differences. Just as you may laugh at stories of American tourists abroad who were stunned to discover people who don't speak English or trade in dollars, you can laugh at the stories of talk show panelists who forgot they were engaged before vast, unseen audiences in a conversation, debate, or argument.

In a conversation, even one that's not particularly argumentative, it's not unusual for one participant to call an opponent's statement into question, to argue context and assumptions, or even to insist that a statement is false. What happens in the broadcast studio is no different. The guests who get into trouble are intimidated by their surroundings, nervous about talking in public, or concerned about ingratiating themselves with the host. This isn't the U.S. Army. The host is not the general, and the guests are not privates. They are equals. It is not only permissible, but frequently necessary, for a guest to challenge a host's statements, and even to refuse to answer a question as presented.

Some people, even lawyers, make the mistake of comparing a one-on-one broadcast interview to a courtroom proceeding. A broadcast interview is structured, but it does not have legal ground rules. In the courtroom, a witness must answer the questions of the unfriendly lawyer. But if that lawyer goes off base, the witness's counsel will rise to his defense and call a foul. He will object to leading, irrelevant, immaterial, and any other kind of question that falls beyond what is permissible and reasonable. Then the friendly lawyer will get up and question his client in a way that brings out a more favorable side of the story. In a broadcast interview, the subject must be his own defense lawyer. And if he doesn't assume that role, he's in trouble.

Be reminded of what happened to Chesterfield Smith when he failed to act as his own counsel. Asked what the odds were for getting a good lawyer, he proceeded to plot them. Even if the answer to that reporter's question on *Meet the Press* was knowable, it wasn't quantifiable, at least not in those terms. The witness stand is not a good model for a broadcast interview, and some questions dare not be answered as they're framed. An alert guest must remember that.

For instance, the participant in one of my practice sessions was a highly placed executive in another of the world's largest oil companies. The interview had been tough but fair for the first four or five minutes. Then the host rolled out the following grenade:

> I find it peculiar that during the late sixties and early seventies, you people were telling yourselves that a fuel shortage was coming. You were telling the government that a shortage was coming. But in

your advertising, you were telling an unsuspecting public to drive *more!* To buy more! To consume excessively!

Was that irresponsibility due to greed or ineptness?

We switched to a tight shot of the executive's face as he blanched perceptibly. Was he thinking of an answer at all, or planning a hideous exile for the company's PR man who got him into this mess?

After about three seconds of awful silence, which somehow seemed longer (especially to him), the nimble reply came forth: "I guess it was ineptness, Roger."

It is folly to let the pressure of the moment force you into an either/or, yes/no, true/false quiz when neither of the choices really serves your purpose or conveys your position.

Let us inspect the carnage here, and reconstruct the edifice, if possible.

In responding to an A or B question, there are four options available, not merely two. The others are both and neither.

"It was neither greed nor ineptness, Roger, because we devised a plan to alleviate the situation, and we sought the government's support—but without success. Had we prevailed, the crises of the seventies could have been averted."

"A Stanley Cup or a profit?" It's too late to save Bottom Line Cohen, but the answer is both. Or maybe it's yes. The history of professional sports is replete with evidence that winning tends to be a lucrative proposition. "Fan support is intensified," Cohen might have said. "The Garden sells out more frequently. The cash register rings, enabling us to increase our expenditures for player development. Championship teams and profitable operations are Siamese twins." And so on.

But that's mostly playing defense. Don't forget the offense, too. If you've come on a program to promote life, liberty and the pursuit of happiness, don't be impaled on the following prongs, "Which is more important to save mankind—guns or butter?" You may deem it unfortunate, but guns and butter aren't mutually exclusive (like life and death). "A supply of both commodities in a dangerous, hungry world enhances the larger good of life, liberty, and the pursuit of happiness...," after a 15 word preface, life, liberty and the pursuit of happiness have replaced guns and butter on the oral agenda, and you're in charge of the conversation once again.

Stay in charge!

chapter eleven
The Absent Party Question

Remember when you were little, your mother told you not to say anything behind someone's back that you wouldn't say to his face? There's a corollary in television and radio. Say anything you like about your opponent's positions, his illogical assumptions, his useless conclusions, his insubstantial arguments. But never question your opponent's motives, his sincerity, or his devotion to a cause, especially when he or she isn't present. You weren't the only one who got that lecture from your mother. We all dislike the person who attacks an absent party.

HOST: Doctor, I agree with you that medicine has the most capable and dedicated professionals in the world. But if that's so, why is the Teddy Kennedy faction of the Democratic Party out to get you?

PHYSICIAN: I'll tell you why. Because our Chappaquiddick friend wants to be president of the United States, and he doesn't give a damn who he steps on to get there. He doesn't care about health care delivery. He just wants a hot issue.

The doctor may have found that exchange personally therapeutic, and his friends and colleagues may congratulate him on a shiv well wielded. But how does it appear to the audience out there, eager to understand the issue of national health insurance and willing to let this discussion help form an opinion? Terrible, that's how. They see a man kneecapped who isn't even present to defend himself. Don't attribute ugly motives to your opponent. It makes the audience question your motives and consequently distrust your position.

Nonetheless, questions about people who aren't present keep coming, partly because they're a wonderful device for perpetuating a debate.

Monday

> HOST: Recently, Mr. Hot-Blooded Consumer Activist said the labor movement is the single greatest cause of inflation in America. How do you respond to that?
>
> AGING LABORITE: This isn't the first time he's been out of his depth. He should stick to supermarket issues and stay out of labor economics.

Wednesday

> HOST: Mr. Laborite says you're not qualified to discuss inflation. (Note the casual misrepresentation.) Is it an area you feel you should stay out of?
>
> HOT-BLOOD: Of course not. I don't know exactly what Laborite meant, but I do know that before his advanced years began to take their awful toll, there was great mutual respect and admiration between consumers and the labor movement.

The interviewer ignited an inflammatory debate at the expense of two guests who never laid eyes on each other. Hot-Blooded, in particular, made the mistake of accepting a paraphrasing of what Laborite said. It sounded like an insult, so he slung one back. If a so-called quote is out of context, and you're not familiar with it, there is no reason to accept its veracity at face value. There are all kinds of ways to sidestep such situations. You can make a mitigating remark ("I find it hard to believe that he said this but, if he did, I certainly can't agree because...."), or you can simply address the issue and ignore the personal aspersions. Or you can take the hard line: defer the answer until you have seen the exact quote, context and all, for yourself.

It is amusing to read both exchanges together, but there is no guarantee that the audience for Monday's program is the same as the audience for Wednesday's. Even if it were, how many would remember as they watched on Wednesday exactly what was said on Monday? You can't assume that an audience knows anything more than you are providing at the moment, which explains why television and radio incessantly recapitulate.

Of course, it's also possible that an absent person did say something as bad as it sounds, so you don't want your response to be evasive. Just don't be suckered into making a remark you'll later regret.

Speaking of suckering, it is easy in retrospect to ridicule Jane Fonda for the turbulent excesses of her youth. But there was a time in the sixties and seventies when she spoke for a passionate constituency on certain public issues, not only the Vietnam War, but also on the commercial applications of nuclear power. Utility executives would retch at the mention of her name.

Things like passion and retching make for wonderful television, so I for one never missed an opportunity in my private workshops to bait the utility industry with Ms. Fonda's expert testimony.

HOST: If Jane Fonda is so wrong about nuclear power, why would she interrupt and possibly damage a lucrative movie career to rabble-rouse in the streets?

UTILITY BIGGIE: Listen, nitwit, that Fonda broad is part of the Hard Left conspiracy. We call it the Lunatic Fringe. She's really promoting socialism, or worse—and it's incompatible with capitalism. That means she's undermining free enterprise and destroying America.

I missed it if Jane Fonda ever was indicted at the time by the Justice Department for treason, but that's beside the point. Presumably it was this utility executive's intention in that debate to make converts, not harden polarity. Fans of a fine actress might be persuaded to differ with her views on complicated issues where she is perceived to lack credentials and credibility. And it's still possible for the same people to remain fans and admirers.

Adherents to Ms. Fonda's views, or anyone else's, come in at least three shapes: (1) firmly committed, (2) mostly committed, and (3) generally committed. Lure the latter group (or part of it) away from her as a result of a public discussion and your own constituency is presumably enlarged. Drive them back into the pack and your opponent's hold is strengthened. That's called c–o–u–n–t–e–r–p–r–o–d–u–c–t–i–v–e, notwithstanding the pleasures of personal therapy. Following is a better answer:

UTILITY BIGGIE: Jane Fonda is a swell actress, and none of us will ever forget "Barbarella." But she *isn't* a physicist. I am. And I can tell you without equivocation....

It's the difference between heat and light.

chapter twelve
The Loaded Preface

Sometimes in a talk show or interview situation a perfectly legitimate question will go sour: "Given the low regard in which the business community is held, why would anyone getting out of college want to go into banking?"

Fair enough, albeit distasteful. Repeated polls of the public have shown that business in general is not highly esteemed or overly admired. At least it is not in the same class with Mother Teresa and Will Rogers.

But the insertion of just one little adverb can throw the same question off course: "Given the *deservedly* low regard in which the business community is held, why would anyone getting out of college want to go into banking?" (Listen carefully!)

Suddenly one question has become two issues. If the guest, a local banker, has come on the program to explain the opportunities in his profession, he has a choice. (Although it's established that business is not generally esteemed, it is conjecture at best that such a reputation is deserved.) He can focus on the word *deservedly* at the risk of marching into a cul-de-sac whence he will never return. Or he can dismiss the charge and bridge to his own point. (Ignoring the word deservedly is to lend credence to the allegation.) The trick is to defuse the insult clearly, but also foreclose it and move away in a determined and forceful manner so that further probes are squelched.

Frequently it is possible to anticipate loaded statements, as American League batters learned to anticipate the Vaseline pitch from Catfish Hunter. If so, prepare your defenses. Preparation doesn't mean just getting your side of the story straight. It also means anticipating the arguments and contentions of the opposition. If, for example, our friendly banker knew that his counterpart on the program was the Socialist Party's candidate for mayor, he could have anticipated something like this: "We all know that businessmen are the most corrupt lawbreakers since Butch Cassidy and the Sundance Kid. How can you muster the gall to invite young people to join you?" The phrasing is vastly different but the charge is roughly the same, and so is the danger. If the banker is to get to the business he came to conduct, he can't waste time in a senseless sparring match about comparative morality.

If there is one question you dread being asked, rest assured (or uncomfortably) that it will be asked. And woe to the man or woman who does not have an answer prepared. In both of the above-mentioned cases, the banker could have used a variation on a standard reply. He could have anticipated that a question about ethics and esteem would come up and, knowing his host or fellow panelists, he might have anticipated it wrapped and ribboned in a loaded preface. The banker could acknowledge that some people feel that business has betrayed the public confidence, although he personally feels that the business community as a whole should not be held accountable for the acts of a few any more than another recognizable group should be branded for the acts of a minority of its members: "But because some people feel negatively about the business community, it's even more important to recruit bright, eager and idealistic youngsters into the world of business and banking, where they can contribute the kind of leadership that business needs in the future...." And just as suddenly, the conversation is right where the banker wants it again.

An irascible banker might be tempted to respond less genteelly to the candidate from the Socialist Party, and that's okay, too (this is not a sport for wimps), with one proviso: start with the counter-insult; don't conclude with it. Put distance in a dissertation between the heat and light of which we have spoken. In most instances the dialogue will flow and continue from the conclusion of your answer, not the preamble. A cantankerous businessman might commence as follows: "You'll see it convincingly demonstrated on Election Day how few people feel as you do, but even so, you raise a salient point...."

Also, there is a difference between a loaded preface and a false premise. A few years ago, before he retired after an illustrious career as chairman of Citicorp, Walter Wriston obviously had anticipated the hard questions on a Sunday morning network show:

REPORTER: Mr. Wriston, I would like to ask you something about the banking business. There is a growing number of people who believe that the banking industry exercises too much power over our economic life. As head of one of the largest and most powerful financial institutions, how do you respond to that charge?

WRISTON: You say there is a growing number of people who say that. I frankly have very little evidence that that is the fact.

The banking business is the most fragmented major industry in the United States. The largest bank in the country has less than five percent market share. I would doubt whether any other industry is so fragmented.

Secondly, there are 14,600 banks in the United States serving communities across the country, and the biggest power is exercised where there is no competition. But the facts are that today the relative power of the banks has declined.

I will give you a specific example. The first loan I ever made on airplanes was (for) a DC-3 that cost $125,000. The legal limit of our bank at that time—we could finance about ten. Today an aircraft costs around $25,000,000, and a single bank can finance only about four.

So, relatively, they have not kept up as fast as they should with the growth in our economy.

No matter how loaded or false the question, there is always a way to disarm it, but the interviewee must anticipate that someone will ask it. He can disarm it by disagreeing with the loaded part of the premise, or by acknowledging that some people may feel that way. But then he can proceed to his own point via a swift bridge

113

before his adversaries have a chance to turn the discussion in their direction. No matter how carefully you review all the possible ways you can be challenged, it is probably impossible to guarantee no surprises, however. Just be as careful as you can, and then stay alert during the show.

All this is good advice for a polite, civilized talk show. But what happens when the opposition is not polite? What happens when they interrupt and refuse to be interrupted themselves?

When such an exchange begins, the person who starts the attack, who first loads the question and boorishly interrupts the answer, is generally seen as the villain (the bully) by the audience at home. Make sure this point is firmly established. Let the person interrupt you two times before you make a real move. Some panelists will take advantage of your good manners and shout you down every time you start to score a telling point. Let them get away with it exactly twice, which is usually sufficient to establish the offender as a true Philistine.

The third time, lean forward in your chair, smile, and, if you can, press your fingertips against that person's forearm, and say, "Just a moment, please. I wonder if I can finish this point." Your startling movement forward should be enough to throw the person off track, while you continue merrily along. Whatever happens, don't be as rude as your tormentor. Smile graciously as you request the floor.

Finally (in desperation) there are a couple of wicked back alley techniques which can be used on a television show that is dotted with commercial interruptions, as most programs are. (These tactics aren't necessarily recommended, although I've had occasion to use them both with marvelous results!)

Watch the floor director during the commercial breaks. When he or she signals the host to stand-by with anywhere from three to five seconds left before the proceedings resume, turn to the man who has been giving you so much trouble, and whisper softly: "Did you know your fly is open?" If the troublemaker is a woman, tell her she has lipstick on her teeth. If she isn't wearing lipstick, ask her if she knows she has something lodged between her front teeth. Tell her that "it looks like spinach to me." Even if she hasn't eaten spinach since girlhood, it's virtually guaranteed to produce at least 60 seconds of puckering, grimacing, and discomfiture.

And don't forget to smile.

chapter thirteen
Triskaidekaphobia*

For that reason, nothing of substance appears in this space.

---

* That's what it's called if you're uptight about this particular number. Many highrises and hotels omit the 13TH floor because people think it's unlucky. We're taking no chances with this book either.

chapter fourteen

Outnumbered!

Okay class, we have focused so far on meeting the press in ones or twos, often on television and radio. Now let's meet the press en masse, also a scary prospect, and sometimes ill advised for reasons soon to be enumerated. But there are exceptions.

Call the press together (and hope they come to the party) when your story is best told at length, when open-ended and freewheeling questioning will enhance it.

Call them all together as an economy of scale when time or other commitments don't permit the scheduling of 40 separate interviews or visitations.

Especially call a press conference when something that you cherish must be seen to be believed and appreciated: for purposes of exhibition or demonstration.

I don't know how the following data were determined, but the compendium has been published in so many journals that I hesitate to refute it; I've even come to accept it (as per the partial citation in chapter 2).

It says here in the fine print that one percent of what we learn in life is through tasting, 1½ percent is through touching, 3½ percent through smelling, 11 percent through hearing, and 83 percent through seeing.

Moreover, we the people (including the press) are alleged to retain 10 percent of what we read, 20 percent of what we hear, 30 percent of what we see, and 50 percent of what we see and hear. (It may be unnecessarily confusing to note that some of what we see is also what we read.)

If there is any validity here (and if you remember more than 10 percent of it) you may conclude something like the following:

> For purposes of mass communication, a press conference (where the principals can be seen and heard) is more effective than a press release. (However, if you elect to call a press conference, don't underestimate the importance of tasting. Lots of reporters show up to freeload.)

However, if you elect to call a press conference (Does this sentence seem redundant? Do you remember why?) expect any or all of the following to occur:

- Many reporters who promise to attend, won't,
- including the most important reporters from the most important places.
- Of those present, many will be late; others will leave early,
- and crews from the television and radio fraternity will be disruptive.
- Of those who remain for the hors d'oeuvres or lunch, many will be bizarrely dressed, others will smell like Olympic hammer throwers, and at least a few will have studied table manners under the eighth century Vikings.

How does it sound so far?

In general, press conferences are poorly attended because reporters regard them as nuisances (some press conferences are outright ruses) and many conferences are convened at awkward times or in inconvenient places.

By contrast, Ralph Nader's news conferences in the 50s and 60s were successes for two reasons: he always had a revelation to announce (whether or not it eventually held water), and he called them on Saturday mornings, a slow news day, thereby increasing attendance. Strictly on merit, Mr. Nader didn't deserve to become as famous as he has, and mostly he owes his notoriety to a dubious decision by General Motors, which hired a flatfoot to follow him around. That made him seem important, a man wronged and, as a result, irresistible to the press: a David badgered and harassed by Goliath, a man of the people shadowed and intimidated by the Establishment. It had the essential components for a fascinating, continuing story: characters (abundantly), drama, and conflict. Of course, in achieving fame, it also helped immeasurably that Mr. Nader was totally dedicated and exceedingly strange. His picture doesn't appear in the dictionary next to the words *paranoid* and *relentless,* but someday it might.

Gleaning and Preening

Thanks to John F. Kennedy (who started it all on January 25, 1961), presidential press conferences are better attended than others. No, Mr. Kennedy didn't invent the conferences, but he was the first U.S. president to allow television cameras (an idea whose time had come) forever altering this particular genre. In a previous age, reporters met periodically with presidents to glean information. Now they meet to be seen on national television in the gleaning process and, accordingly, attendance has skyrocketed. In hopes of a chance to stand and recite for the American people, journalists are preening more than ever before, crafting one momentous question which eventually will be memorized or transcribed on an index card to be held in trembling hands. Rumpled suits are cleaned and pressed for these occasions; new dresses are purchased. And one network anchorman, formerly a White House correspondent, even vocalized in the shower to improve the timbre of his voice for these prime time performances.

If your press conference isn't similarly well attended, don't take it personally. At the White House, the primary attraction isn't the president, although he's several cuts above anyone else who comes to mind. It's principally the cameras from the television networks.

What I'm saying is that press conference enticements are essential, and a Bacchanalian buffet table is sometimes sufficient to lure hungry reporters, for instance. News organizations are eminently frugal, and most of their minions are resourceful to a fault. So consider refreshments, sparing those in attendance the necessity of buying their own lunches, brunches, and cocktails.

Junkets sometimes work, too, provided the trip or experience is exotic or unusual enough. (A trek to Secaucus to see your boiler works won't attract as many reporters as a gondola ride, all expenses paid, in Venice.)

I belabor this point about attendance for a fundamental reason: where the press is deployed is what the press will cover. If reporters and camera crews are dispatched for two hours on a Saturday morning to a Ralph Nader conference, notwithstanding its actual newsworthiness, the Nader conference will receive disproportionate coverage. (This is a business, remember?)

Having somehow connived an acceptable throng into attending, press conferences, like Gaul, are usually divided into three parts (make it four parts if the above-mentioned refreshments are served afterwards).

First are the formal presentations, hopefully something more than droning speeches. Films, videotapes, slides, charts, and performing pandas are some of the possibilities to liven up the proceedings. Also, because the press has been spoiled after decades of toadying by the public relations fraternity, most reporters in attendance will expect you or your PR man to have done much of their work in advance. As a class, reporters are notably lazy and inattentive at press conferences; some will take a few notes, others won't. That means the complete texts of your prepared remarks and presentations should be included in the press kit that you distribute beforehand or afterwards to every man, woman, and child within range, along with the appropriate photographs, charts, and a press release (a distillation of the important messages and central points being communicated here, written in the form of a news story). Sometimes a few paragraphs are sufficient. Most press releases aren't longer than two or three pages of double-spaced typing. (A so-called press kit is nothing more than a folder containing the materials that you hope to see in the next day's newspapers and on television.)

Incidentally, start the first phase of your conference at the appointed time or after a grace period of no more than 10 minutes. Don't wait for the crew that you think is en route from *CBS News.* Doing so is affrontery of the first magnitude to the punctual in your assemblage, who you don't want to annoy more than necessary.

The second part of your conference is called *Q & A*, which, of course, stands for questions and answers. (It's also called Christian versus lions, and all the rules and directives previously explained about preparation and performance are still in force.) If you want the Q & A to be a Chinese fire drill, merely say at the conclusion of your formal presentation that you (and maybe others of your associates) will "now take questions from the floor." If you want to retain a modicum of control, announce the rules and procedures beforehand. "One at a time, please. Just raise your hand and I'll call on you in turn. The conference won't end until everyone has been accommodated."

If you are pressed for time and must limit the question period, specifically announce that stricture at the outset so no one will think that you ran for cover at the first threat of high winds and heavy weather.

Q & A is furthermore the trickiest part of a press conference. It is also central and the most important. Among the tricks for you to master are the following:

A. Regardless of how extraneous the questions may seem, find ways in your answers to repeat and restate the principal theme(s) from your formal presentation. (The bridging technique is fully applicable.)

B. In the likely event that a few reporters (or other people in the hall) are friends or acquaintances of yours, it may be possible to plant several questions (the ones you dearly would love to answer) in advance. (As Louis Pasteur once said: "Chance favors the *prepared* man." Leave nothing to it.)

C. If no one else will perform the above-mentioned service, ask yourself those questions. After answering one from the floor, and before you acknowledge the next raised hand, say something like this: "One of the basic questions here is...." And having asked it (aloud), it's probably incumbent upon you to answer (aloud). Then point at the next reporter.

D. Maintain steady eye contact with each questioner as he or she poses a query. If a question is especially friendly or easy, also continue eye contact with the reporter who asked it throughout your answer, and particularly at the end of your answer. (That may prompt or encourage a follow-up question from the same person, who, we already have established, is no threat to your sanctity. The second question may be even friendlier and easier.) If a question is unfriendly (even hostile, or at least skeptical), look away from the interrogator, preferably to the other side of the hall, as you finish your answer. Usually that does two things for you, both beneficial. It prompts a question from someone else within your purview, and prevents you from seeing that your previous tormentor is waving his hand like mad.

E. Don't conclude a Q & A session abruptly or without fair warning. "We have time for three more questions before the caterer demands our presence at lunch. The lady in the red dress in the front row will be first. The man over there from the *Houston Post* is second. And that dashing network correspondent in the burgundy turtleneck will be last. Lady in red?"

The third part of a press conference is the mingling afterwards, which is really an extension of the second part, since the Q & A inevitably will continue, less formally. Don't leave the room abruptly, and remember that you remain on stage and on the record for as long as you stay. (In this phase, the television and radio people may want to take you aside for individual interviews in succession. Maybe the writers, too.)

The imbibement period is last (and yours is club soda, unless you're enamored of seeing a drunken outburst in tomorrow's headlines). You are still on stage and on the record.

The next day in the press, your story will be multifariously screwed up, which is why the papers run corrections and editor's notes.

124

Outnumbered!

Eric Sevareid, quoting Walter Lippman in a published essay, explains why.

The central point is not that the full truth is revealed in any one account, but that out of free reporting and discussion, truth emerges.

It takes time. And a fairly long attention span. If a story is 50 percent wrong the first day, it's probably 85 percent right the second, and 99 percent the third. The news tends to correct itself. And it's the only institution that advertises attacks upon itself. How do we hear about the inadequacies of the press except through the press?

About covering the likes of presidential press conferences, Mr. Sevareid added the following:

What's the big difference between electronic and print journalism? It's in this business of covering things live, publishing events as they happen. That's a quantum leap. Most people who criticize broadcasting don't seem to grasp this simple fact. And they don't appreciate the extreme difficulty of doing it well. Imagine a columnist willing to sit at his typewriter and start off a review of a presidential speech as the man is talking, and having it finished and published instantaneously.

If some of that sounds like apologia, Eric Sevareid is nevertheless largely on target. Covering you and what you say isn't as easy as it looks. But the press will get the story straight, eventually, with your help on the phone the next day.

Is that the bell? Class is dismissed.

chapter fifteen
On the Record

That's what you are whenever you meet the press, formally or informally, professionally or socially. What you say and do, and what they infer (or both), are apt to be reported to the public, complete with your name, rank, and serial number. Unless otherwise specified in advance, you are deemed to be teetering on the top rung of the journalistic ladder of freedom. You are on the record, in other words. Newsmen are in no way limited or restricted in using your remarks and material, including direct quotations, fully attributed to you by name and affiliation.

However, there are four lower rungs on the same ladder, and a news sophisticate such as you are becoming should understand the differences. There are conditions that may be imposed before you speak, which somehow restrict or constrain the reporter's handling of the information disseminated. The restrictions range from subtle to severe, and many reporters don't understand the full distinctions. It's advised that you clarify same before sermonizing, and gain the reporter's consent. Most of the time, this assures that the two (or more) of you will be playing by the same rules in your forthcoming conversation.

For instance, if you happen to be the pope or the president of the United States, you can successfully invoke the *indirect quotation rule*. (Lesser mortals probably can't.) Here a newsman can attribute comments to you by name in his eventual story, but he can't use quotation marks to indicate that a given statement is verbatim. It's somewhat controversial in journalistic circles on the premise that world leaders should be fully accountable and responsible for what they say, even offhandedly. But it also recognizes that potentates are mortals, too, given occasionally to saying dumb things, sometimes inflammatory and even incorrect things. Grave consequences can result from slips of the tongue, so many super-biggies refuse to talk openly to the press unless they can disclaim their own boo-boos and outbursts. Looking back at newspaper coverage from the first half of the 20TH century, this explains why so few comments are attributed in quotation marks to the likes of Woodrow Wilson, Herbert Hoover, Franklin Roosevelt, Harry Truman, and other leaders.

Next is what's called *euphemistic-source attribution*, and here you may qualify in the judgment of a newsman who is eagerly pursuing a scoop. Maybe you're ratting on your boss, and you don't have a new job lined up. Your condition for spilling the beans about environmental abuses at the plant site is to constrain the reporter from using your name in his exposé. (It's the beans he wants anyway, so usually he'll agree.) Here you become a highly reliable source, or a spokesman for the firm who requested anonymity.

As Secretary of State for Richard Nixon, Henry Kissinger used this ploy all the time for floating trial balloons. Comments attributed in the press to a senior official on the Secretary's plane (or words to that effect) were usually the comments of Dr. Kissinger himself, but the Prince of Peace could later disavow them if he didn't like what he saw in cold type.

Fourth is the so-called Lindley Rule, and if you think I'm exaggerating when I say that many reporters don't comprehend these subtle distinctions, ask the next one you meet to define the Lindley Rule. (Unless he or she resides in Washington, he or she won't know. In exactly two more sentences, you will be in a position to explain it.) Is was named for Ernest K. Lindley, an editor at *Newsweek*. In short, it says that a newsman can use the totality of what you tell him, but with no attribution whatsoever, even to highly reliable you. It is infrequently used except when the federal government is leaking classified information, because it gives the appearance that the whole story was dreamed up by the writer of the article (which occasionally happens). It is regarded by the fourth estate as a reasonable journalistic procedure, helpful in prying the lids off juicy stories but, like the indirect quotation rule, it is rarely invoked outside of the Washington Beltway.

Fifth (and most extreme) is off the record, where a reporter who agrees in advance to such an arrangement is completely gagged. The cloak of secrecy remains intact, and violation is regarded as original sin. It's frequently bureaucrats seeking to curry favor with the press who tattle off the record. However, the danger here is the following: While a reporter can't use the information, now he knows about it, which may enable him to ferret the same story from someone else who imposes only the Lindley Rule. Voila! The lid is off. And your boss or associates may give you suspicious looks for the balance of your professional career (which may be short).

Grizzled veterans of these wars offer the forthcoming advice, and I'll cite the comments of Michael Korda: "It is important to remember that a journalist's job is to *get* a story. He or she cannot ignore what you have said as if you never said it. There are complex rules" (see the preceding) "but in general, if you know something you don't want to see in the newspapers, don't talk about it!"

There is one other term which you may have heard: *for background only.* We have covered it above. Anything on background is really the Lindley Rule. It says to a reporter: "Know what I tell you, but don't attribute it to me," and it's commonly employed when a person of importance or vulnerability is discussing a matter in circumstances where his or her name cannot be used for reasons of public policy or personal safety. Also, it is frequently abused by persons intending to sink a knife or do a number on someone without risking their own positions or facing the music themselves. It forbids a reporter from any source identification, even the euphemistic kind like "a representative of the firm who refuses to be identified."

Presumably it is unnecessary for me to add that all of this rigmarole about rules and conditions is applicable only to private (or closed) conversations with reporters. It is exceedingly difficult for you to invoke the Lindley Rule or go off the record on the *CBS Evening News* in front of 10,000,000 people.

But if you pull it off, please let me know how.

chapter sixteen

A Baker's Dozen

Andy Warhol once said that all of us are destined to become famous for 15 minutes. Achieving such fame or notoriety, even for longer periods, was the main theme of an essay in a business publication by Art Stevens, a New York PR man. One of the tips on Art's list was to "write 10 articles a year in your name." (Nine more will suffice for Mr. Stevens.) He said, "This is such an obvious way to achieve visibility for you and your company—and your successes— that I have always been surprised that so few people consider this option. Pick out 10 publications that reach your target audience, including daily newspapers in your area, consumer magazines and trade publications."

It is good advice for at least two reasons that Mr. Stevens neglects to reveal.

First, if you want the press to blaze a trail to your doorstep, it is imperative for you to be identified with a cause or expertise of your very own, real or perceived, such as Richard Nixon on world affairs, Ralph Nader on consumerism, Art Stevens on visibility, Hyman Rickover on submarines, or Andy Warhol on soup cans. Authoritative writings on that subject of choice can effectively implant the perception of your wisdom and inscrutability, especially when your articles appear in the national journals, for instance on the op-ed pages of *The New York Times*, *The Washington Post*, and *The Wall Street Journal*. (The latter is not a parochial comment, which you may have concluded if you live and work in

Omaha, Nebraska. Those New York and Washington-based papers are widely circulated to editors and broadcasters in the hinterlands, too.) *Newsweek* magazine runs a column called "My Turn," where the views of outsiders are published. Someday it should be your turn.

This writing gambit nets a primary audience of newspaper and magazine readers (which is not inconsiderable), and is equally beneficial for its secondary ramification, namely TV and radio exposure. Although few broadcasters will freely confess to the following without a massive injection of sodium pentothal, it's an indisputable fact that TV and radio people are irrationally, unduly, and disproportionately influenced by what appears in the newspapers (particularly the prestigious ones). It must be news, or it must be important, they reason, because Max Frankel *(Times)* and Ben Bradlee *(Post)* decided to print it. (That behavior is the result of two factors: respect for one's elders and a deeply ingrained inferiority complex. Television and radio are nouveau riche. Movable type was invented in the 15TH century.)

We previously determined that the quickest and most pervasive way to stardom in America is via television, so next you may get a call from a local talk show or the *20/20* people at *ABC News*, where the staff has been clipping your arresting and provocative articles. "We're doing a segment about soup cans," they will explain on the phone, "and we'd like you for an interview, please."

Another tip on the Art Stevens PR list is actually two tips in the same paragraph: "Get to know the media" and "There is no need to be in awe of the media."

The media include the press, and media and press people are mostly less than formidable or majestic. They are everyday men and women who realize disappointments, triumphs, and frustrations, not unlike you. (Everyone's football coach once said: "They put their pants on one leg at a time.") Two or three mornings a week I ride the same 6:15 train to town with Andy Rooney of *60 Minutes*, who looks and behaves himself like any other businessman on the platform. Except for the fact that Mr. Rooney muses about doorknobs or junk yards on Sunday evenings for approximately two minutes on CBS, you wouldn't notice him in a crowd, and at 6:15 in the morning, he is grateful not to be noticed or bothered. Rooney is shorter than most of his fellow riders, somewhat overweight, and dressed more dumpily than most of the Wall Street types; he grumbles like the rest of us when the train is late, appears from his facial expressions to suffer acute gastric distress, and immerses himself en route in the morning papers like everyone else.

When Mr. Stevens advises that you "get to know the media," he is suggesting in part that you get to know persons like Andy Rooney who happen to work for news organizations (just as other people happen to work for haberdashers and travel agents). Knowing their beats is important; knowing something about their penchants and personalities is helpful, too.

In journalism, a beat is tantamount to an ongoing assignment: City Hall, the police station, business, ladies' garments, pro football, and so on. On the mass medium of television, where time is short and precious, fewer abstruse and peripheral beats are regularly covered by reporters. Mostly their focus is on what you might term the front-page news of the day. (In the frequent absence of our own jargon, those of us in the television business borrow liberally and shamelessly from newspapers and the print media. That accounts for Dan Rather being called the managing editor of the *CBS Evening News*. On the BBC in Great Britain, he would, more correctly, be called a *news reader*.) Walter Cronkite said, as I noted, that the whole script for a typical newscast would fill less than three columns on the front page of your morning paper. With that much limitation and constraint, it isn't feasible or worthwhile for television and radio reporters to be assigned exclusively to aviation news or the Securities and Exchange Commission, so it follows that most people in broadcast news are generalists. (Of course there are exceptions, particularly in Washington, where each of the networks has a correspondent stationed all day long at the White House, the State Department, and so on.) A general assignment reporter in broadcasting is expected to be adept and competent, no matter where his boss may send him to cover an event.

Also, it is important to reiterate that TV is the mass medium of communications, and network television must lure the national mass of available viewers. Generally that rules out any extended or regular coverage of esoteric topics. Whereas *The New York Times* can publish 18 pages of wine news every Thursday, those of us on the 6:15 train can skip over it to the sports pages if we aren't interested in the Napa Valley or the Gallo brothers. But due to the linear nature of television, skipping is impossible; the entire audience is forced to wait, and Americans don't take kindly to waiting. Our attention spans are said to be short. When TV viewers switch to another channel or turn off their sets, television broadcasters know the ultimate form of rejection, which generally leads to unemployment. Two rules therefore govern procedure in TV: keep it moving and make sure it's interesting to the majority.

Following are some good-natured descriptions of the top-flight people in network television from whom Americans in droves get their news and information. Any of these personalities who keep it moving and make it interesting can help you become lavishly famous, or notorious. I did a similar profiling exercise several years ago for a newspaper syndicate, and I am stunned looking back at my previous work. Almost half of my former subjects aren't currently active, which proves that attrition and mortality are factors in broadcasting, too.

Back then, David Frost ("Captain Jet Lag") and Dick Cavett ("The Little Engine That Could") were holding forth for the umpteenth time on PBS. Walter Cronkite (now retired), John Chancellor (now a pundit), and Frank Reynolds (now deceased) were the principal anchormen on CBS, NBC, and ABC, respectively. Bill Monroe and George Herman were the moderators of *Meet the Press* and *Face the Nation*. Daniel Schorr worked for CNN. Tom Snyder hosted something called *Tomorrow* at NBC. Rona Barrett was included, so were Mike Douglas, Merv Griffin, David Susskind, Bernard Kalb, Irving R. Levine, Edwin Newman, Tom Pettit, and Max Robinson (among others), none of whom now appears as frequently (or at all) on the teeny, flickering screen. (Martin Agronsky was on my previous list. Nowadays his TV exposure is limited to once a week bull sessions for 30 minutes with the likes of Hugh Sidey and

Carl Rowan about what's wrong in Washington. For that purpose, 30 minutes is rarely enough time.)

At these levels of professional stature and accomplishment, broadcasting isn't a revolving door. Attrition has occurred, and TV stars aren't exempt.

So you needn't get to know or prepare to meet many of the above-mentioned as you contemplate your network interview debut. But if that's the good news, following is the bad: Mike Wallace is still on duty, as are Ed Bradley, Morley Safer, Sam Donaldson, Ted Koppel, David Brinkley, Barbara Walters, David Hartman, Bryant Gumbel, Dan Rather, Phil Donahue, Roger Mudd, and Tom Brokaw (known in certain circles as "Duncan the Wonder Horse").

When you face them for the first time, your effectiveness will be compromised if you revere them, or choke. It was Joseph P. Kennedy, as a young man, who always imagined that his elders in business conferences were clad in long johns, nothing more. It put him at ease, even bemused him. (Tycoons wear long johns, I suppose, especially in Boston and especially in January.) Maybe the same tactic will work for you.

Barbara Walters (who usually doesn't wear long johns, no matter what you're imagining) has a weadily wecognizable delivewy which made bitsy speech impediments acceptable on national television. (Therapists call it the W and R substitution.) Most of her guests are sufficiently well mannered not to mention it. However, author Studs Terkel once remarked that appearing on a program with Bah-baw-ah is like being interviewed by Elmer Fudd. In the autumn of an amazing broadcasting career, Ms. Walters spends most of her current air time in the company of cosmic celebrities asking the likes of Barbra Streisand, Katharine Hepburn, and Ronald Reagan if they would rather be trees.

Speaking of impediments, Tom Brokaw has trouble with diphthongs, but no trouble with loftiness. He's also tenacious and persistent in the pursuit of truth, much like a puppy with a rag. But tenacious is different from antagonistic, which is a one word description of Sam Donaldson. No matter which position you stake on a particular issue, he'll stake the polar opposite. (You get first choice, however.)

Mr. Donaldson's Sunday morning pal on *This Week*, David Brinkley, is laconic and courtly, true to his North Carolina heritage. Virtually everything he says on television is delivered wryly, dryly, and wearily.

Phil Donahue and David Hartman are approximately two of a kind: self-depreciating (Donahue) and just plain folks (Hartman). With the latter, it's largely an act. (Mr. Hartman is no patsy.) Donahue says to a guest, "Explain that again. I'm a slow learner." (Don't believe that either.)

Hartman's early morning counterpart is Bryant Gumbel of NBC, another recluse (albeit glib and quick witted) who shines brightest when a camera is pointed in his direction.

Over at *60 Minutes*, I'm saving Mike Wallace for last. (He deserves a chapter for himself.) Ed Bradley, except in the presence of Robin Williams or Lena Horne, is dour and forbidding, as if he'd been given a private view of the apocalypse. He is also intense and essentially humorless on the job. Morley Safer might have been dreamed up by Jimmy Breslin or Damon Runyon. That face is like 40 miles of unpaved road, and he sometimes appears in a rumpled and crumpled state, as if he had spent a week in a freight car. But he, like most of the others, isn't paid for his looks at CBS.

Roger Mudd is urbane and mostly frustrated. He waited forever as second banana for Walter Cronkite to retire, only to be screwed by CBS when Dan Rather won the anchor job. Mudd left in a huff for NBC, where he was screwed again by the emergence of Brokaw. (Roger's sphere of movement and expertise is Washington, D.C., and his career was somewhat retarded because he always refused to leave town.)

Early in Ted Koppel's run on *Nightline*, TV critics zeroed in on the fact that he looks like the "What, Me Worry?" character from *Mad* magazine. Maybe that diverted their attention from other facts: Koppel is a competent, intelligent journalist with a commanding, forceful delivery.

Dan Rather is something of a journalistic *Rocky.* He hit bottom after a press conference flap with President Nixon in 1974, only to become the heavyweight champion of the world in 1981 (after Cronkite was forced to abdicate). Says Charles Kuralt about Rather, "I recognize that anchormen *can be* brilliant as well as beautiful."

These personalities have at least three things in common: humble to modest origins, above average charisma, and a consuming passion to excel. Mostly they have sacrificed everything else in life to get where they are and to stay there.

But to clumsily paraphrase President Roosevelt, you have nothing to fear from them but fear itself, unless your line of work is nefarious or disgusting.

chapter seventeen

"Mike Fright"

Hardly anyone is immune. Even I matched wits one Sunday with Mike Wallace on *60 Minutes,* although Mike had the last word because his interviews are filmed in advance, and drastically edited (mostly conforming to the producer's preconceptions).

Mike and I mixed it up in front of his cameras and mine for almost an hour. The typewritten transcript is 46 pages long. On the eventual program, five of my comments were used from pages 13 and 14 of the transcript: 14 short sentences. Another five sentences appeared from the bottom of page 16 and the top of 17, two more from page 22 (run completely out of context), and one sentence each from pages 35 and 36. In all, after an hour of talking to Mike, I was permitted to utter a grand total of 207 words on a program seen by millions of viewers nationwide. That may fit your definitions of selectivity or distortion. Still, I have no complaints because the heavy editing came as no surprise. *60 Minutes* is at least consistent, and anyone's option (which I refused) is to decline their overtures.

Well, I have one complaint. But that's getting ahead of my story.

The press is fascinated with so-called media consultants; I think they're secretly flattered (a few are repulsed) that anyone would pay a fee to prepare and be instructed for oral skirmishes with the likes of them. I was disdained one night in 1974 on the *CBS Evening News* by commentator Eric Sevareid, who offered his own tips for interviewees.

SEVAREID: Dress in your normal fashion, act naturally, know your facts, have a sound case, and tell the simple truth.

Later I replied:

HILTON: That's good advice—advice, in fact, we've always included in our curriculum.

But for the uninitiated, there *is* more to it than dressing normally and acting naturally.

One of the differences is that Eric Sevareid has spent decades on television on a nightly basis. You haven't. In that time, he has mostly overcome his anxiety. He is accustomed to the lights, the cameras, the technicians.

Inevitably, his remarks are scripted—yours aren't. His scripts are carefully written, rewritten, put on a teleprompter, rehearsed, taped, and retaped until he gets them right.

Sevareid appears on TV in circumstances which he and CBS completely *control*.

When you get the same opportunity, perhaps your only concern will be to "know your facts."

Subsequently (not unlike F. Lee Bailey while he was defending the Boston Strangler), I have been interviewed over the years by at least five of the television networks (ABC, CBS, NBC, PBS, and CNN), literally hundreds of local TV and radio stations, more than 50 newspapers and magazines, and both of the U.S. wire services.

So it came as no surprise when *60 Minutes* finally called. The producer's name was Grace Diekhaus, and she asked if they could film one of my sessions with a client (to eavesdrop unobtrusively). I promptly agreed, but with one proviso. Sessions with clients aren't mine, I explained to Grace. They're theirs. With a client's permission, I am willing to perform at a Salem Witch Hunt or Yankee Stadium; I have nothing to hide.

Neither do my clients. Nor do most of them want to be exhibited during the process of my ministrations to the American

140

press corps, however. (Mr. Bailey's clients don't devise their defenses and courtroom strategies in the presence of Mike Wallace or *The Washington Post*.) I also mentioned to Grace that *60 Minutes* is about as unobtrusive as the Third Army.

Ms. Diekhaus said she understood, but would I inquire anyway? They wanted to film, she said, on particular days in July at my studio in Manhattan. Several clients were scheduled on our calendar for that week. I told Grace I would talk to them and call her back.

In retrospect, I'm sure my clients thought I was deranged or drunk when I called. (It even crossed my mind at the time.) It was difficult to pose the central question with a straight face: "Would you mind terribly at our upcoming session if Mike Wallace and a crew from *60 Minutes* are present to film it for one of their broadcasts?"

There was stunned silence from two respondents, gales of laughter from the others. One checked his calendar in the middle of my call. (It wasn't April Fool's Day.) Another asked if this was a test. He said, "The session isn't scheduled for several weeks. Have the exercises already begun?" Making a long story as short as possible, they all said thank you for my inquiry, but no thank you, and I reported the results to Grace without identifying anyone.

Okay, she replied, "can Mike interview you?" I said yes, and it was scheduled for a late afternoon in the specified week. They wanted to film, Grace said, at my studio "on the site where your 'classes' are held." I said fine to that, too, and I asked sweetly if we could videotape the proceedings at the same time *60 Minutes* filmed Mike and me. Under the circumstances, Grace could hardly refuse, but she consented without glee, as I recall. In the past, off camera and supposedly off the record remarks by the uninhibited and provocative Mike Wallace had been surreptitiously recorded during *60 Minutes* interviews and inevitably found their way into public print. The program and CBS have been embarrassed more than once, and compelled to apologize.

I told Grace that wasn't my intention. "Television interviews are my business," I explained, and it would be instructive for my purposes to have a complete record of the acknowledged master at work, namely, Mike.

Her concurrence accounts for the fact that I have a 46-page transcript on file, including the off camera and off the record remarks by Wallace and me.

60 Minutes interviews are start and stop affairs. They reload their film cameras every 10 minutes, which interrupts the conversational flow. My tape machines were equipped with 60-minute spools, so we kept running when they stopped. (Like everyone else who works in television, Mike is notably a different person when he thinks the cameras are at rest. I'll explain in a moment.)

Heeding the sage advice contained in chapter four of this book, I shortly set to work in my office to outguess *60 Minutes.* What did they want from me and why? What would be Mike's angle? Of what wrongdoing was I presumed guilty? (If you have watched the program, you know that *60 Minutes* rarely congratulates its subjects.) Moreover, what did I want to accomplish—beyond survival?

After those deliberations in early July, I devised a list of 18 expected questions and rough drafts of my replies, the latter also encompassing points I hoped to score in my own behalf.

In the eventual interview approximately two weeks later, Mike posed 15 of those questions (there were no surprises) including the following one:

WALLACE: Did you "game" this interview before I arrived?

HILTON: Yes. I also "talked it through" with several of my colleagues.

As we finished the interview, Mike inquired (shrewdly) about the questions I anticipated that he didn't ask. I demurred, knowing for sure that CBS's technicians had plenty of film left for their cameras. He had omitted three of the nastiest ones, while covering the more obvious: "Who do you work for?" "What do you charge for your services?" "What do you teach?" "How do you teach it?" And so on.

In the fourth chapter of this book as you prepared for a mythical appearance on *Meet the Press*, I said there wouldn't be time for anyone to ask 25 questions on a half-hour television program. But

60 Minutes, like most interviews which are filmed or taped, is different. There is no time constraint. Mike and I warmed ourselves under the stage lights in my studio for as long as he wanted, which was until he had asked all of his questions and a few more suggested during the film reloadings by Grace Diekhaus.

At the time of the interview, the working title for the segment was "Mike Fright," a play on words. But in the end they decided that was too playful, or maybe too self-serving. It aired on CBS as "Camera Shy," perhaps a reference to my clients who declined to be filmed, although they weren't mentioned on the broadcast.

A popular fiction, which is widely advanced by CBS, is the notion that *60 Minutes* is a news program. It isn't. It's vaudeville. Audiences watch to see the incriminated person get a pie in the face. A serious newsman (who also happens to be a friend of mine) says, "*60 Minutes* is to journalism what *Charley's Angels* was to criminology."

Nevertheless, Mike Wallace is perceived to be the consummate prosecutor on television; the dreaded interrogator. He rarely unmasks in public. Privately he is glib, witty, and loquacious. Publicly, the only face which most of us see, he is stern, assertive, and indefatigable in his search for malfeasance.

Sitting six feet from Mike for a television interview can be an intimidating experience if you aren't girded for it. His eye contact is mostly unbroken. He grimaces incorrigibly for the camera, squinting (skeptically) and arching his eyebrows (disbelievingly). He smirks, but rarely smiles, until a crew member has signaled that the film has run out. It's largely an act and, after 30 years of practice, he's become exceedingly skilled.

But his reputation for excellence is deserved. Unlike others in television and the press, Mike listens intently when his subjects speak. His powers of concentration are impressive. Nuance and subtlety rarely escape his notice. He is intensely curious.

Mike's questions are short, pointed, even blunt.

WALLACE: Just what is it that you do?

HILTON: We explain the television medium and how it works.

WALLACE: To whom?

HILTON: To anyone who has a need to use it.

WALLACE: And the money to pay for your advice?

In tennis parlance (another of Mike's favorite games), these aren't moon balls to the base line, it's volleying at the net. Alertness is key. Staccato thrusts are the most difficult to combat. A pace is established that is intended to stampede the novice. The chances of a misstep or wrong turn are increased. The defense against it is to play what I call opposites. The more rapid-fire Mike's delivery, the more measured and deliberate mine became. The colder he seemed, the warmer I was. The shorter the questions, the lengthier the replies. By the third page of my transcript, less than five minutes into the interview, it became a conversation between us, no longer an interrogation.

If an interviewer is well prepared, if the topic is well researched, and if the questions are abbreviated, the hardship is increased for a respondent. Conversely, the escape routes are numerous when a question is flabby or long winded.

Let's make up an example to illustrate that point. If I wanted to brag on *60 Minutes* about your recent appearance on *Meet the Press* (as a testimony to my coaching), it would be an easy bridge from a general question, and more difficult from a specific one.

INTERVIEWER: Tell us in general terms what *you do* in these television workshops?

That's an open invitation for plaudits at length about you and your astuteness (not to mention mine).

INTERVIEWER: Specifically, what did *you do* last week in your secret session with Leonard Goldenson, the Chairman of ABC?

Both questions cover essentially the same territory: my work and my modus operandi. But the second one is more troublesome

144

because it narrows the range of reply, especially at the outset. At least a preliminary reference to Mr. Goldenson seems to be indicated, lest I appear evasive. And the difficulty is compounded if Goldenson has sworn me to secrecy about our deliberations, which frequently happens with my clients.

One quickly shifts to the other focus of the second question: the secret session.

A possible answer approximates one which I gave to Mike Wallace when he asked for names of the network newscasters whom I have coached (none of whom, I presumed, wanted that kind of publicity). In essence, I said: "As a predicate, you've got to understand my role and function, Mike. I'm not a doctor or lawyer, but there are similes in my view, which my clients seem to appreciate. It's a personal relationship, and a privileged one. Your internist doesn't talk publicly about your condition. A lawyer won't discuss your legal difficulties in the press—not if he wants to *remain* your confidant. And my role, too, is one of confidence. Not secrecy, but privacy—and there *is* a distinction between the two. Whenever my clients release me from that constraint, I'm more than happy to be forthcoming because I need occasional advertising, like any other business."

From there I might have bridged: "For instance, last Sunday on *Meet the Press....*" It would have taken a bit of footwork, but I could have finally gotten around to you!

Evasive? Strictly speaking, yes. There isn't a hint or reference to ABC's former Chairman or the network correspondents. Essentially I said no comment to Mike. But saying it at length, and for some plausible reasons, tends to lessen the audience's suspicion, if not their frustration. Such an answer might be appreciated by viewers who put themselves in my clients' positions and would feel secure in the knowledge that I won't blabber about them either.

One of Mike's angles in our encounter (as surmised) concerned conflicts of interest. For my practice sessions, I employ professional interviewers: friends and acquaintances who work on television and radio. Not in so many words, Mike wanted to know if I thought they were compromised or tainted as a result. Obviously he thought so. At least he did until I inquired about conflicts of his own. (His answer to that question appeared on my tape, but not on his program.)

Notice particularly what he asked me to get the ball rolling, and how:

WALLACE: Who ordinarily sits where I'm sitting?—that is, as the interviewer.

HILTON: *We use probably 12 or 15 different persons, all of whom do shows in television and radio. I think that's very important. However, we don't use news persons.* We use talk show hosts, and persons who *formerly* were news persons.

WALLACE: Well, what if they were to get involved? Is there no potential conflict of interest if all of a sudden on their talk show...no conflict of interest about the possibility of suddenly meeting up with somebody that he has either helped or advised in the past how to answer questions?

HILTON: There is the potential, but let me tell you how we guard against it. We tell our interviewers please not to accept anyone from our courses on their programs at any later time. I'm in no position to *control* what anyone else does, but I don't know of a breach— ever. And we furthermore tell our clients please not to solicit any of the interviewers to go on their shows—and again, I don't know of a breach. I can't control, really, either entity, because I work for my clients and the interviewers are not on my staff, they're free lancers. But I don't know of a breach.

We do one other thing. Our interviewers *don't* instruct. I instruct.

WALLACE: In other words, the interviewers simply bone-up and ask questions?

HILTON: That's right. I don't put anyone except for me in a position to offer advice or the evaluations of a client's performance.

WALLACE: But if the interviewer, nonetheless, is paid by you, and eventually by the client, to sit and ask phony questions...not phony questions, but rehearsed questions, they effectively put themselves out of business as sensible, responsible news people.

HILTON: They're *not* news people.

Remember, please, I was responding in that exchange to the exact wording of Mike's first question: "Who ordinarily sits where I'm sitting?—that is, as the interviewer." We were sitting at the time in my studio; Mike in the interviewer's chair, me in the chair usually reserved for my clients.

Previously, I mentioned to Mike and *60 Minutes*—because it's no particular secret, in fact we promote it—that featured speakers from television and the press are frequently invited (and paid) to address my clients at formal dinners on evenings before our courses begin. Newton Minow (formerly Chairman of the FCC); George Reedy (LBJ's press secretary at the White House, now a Marquette University journalism professor); Floyd Kalber (from NBC's *Today Show* at the time, a personal friend for 20 years); William Small (the CBS bureau chief in Washington, later president of *NBC News*); Sander Vanocur (now of ABC); Edwin Newman (now retired, formerly at *NBC News*); and many others, too, have appeared.

As he posed his next question, I sensed Mike was about to muddy the waters, although none of the above persons had sat in Mike's chair or ever interviewed a client of mine. None had visited my studio, in fact, which isn't where our dinners are held.

WALLACE: Ed Newman. What function does he perform?

HILTON: We have a dinner on the nights before courses begin, and the participants—usually groups of as many as six persons—attend. And we also book someone to speak. It's primarily an "understand-the-media" dinner.

WALLACE: And what does he (Newman) do?

HILTON: He or anyone else makes a short presentation—five or ten minutes—about television and the press and how it works, and responds to questions.

WALLACE: And they are simply—if you will—an attraction?

HILTON: Have you ever been a keynoter at a convention?

WALLACE: I have spoken at conventions.

HILTON: Same role. And I'm sure when you were booked as a speaker, there was a program printed which said, "our speaker tonight—our special guest tonight will be Mike Wallace of CBS News."

WALLACE: Uh-huh. It's true.

His next remark was directed at Grace Diekhaus, who was crouching about ten feet to Mike's right out of the camera's range.

WALLACE: I think Jack's point is reasonably taken. I mean, for instance, I'm going out to Amway in the fall. It's their anniversary. Fiftieth anniversary, whatever the hell it is. And I'm not going to make a speech. I said, "I'll do Q-and-A." For my regular fee. And mind you, I've already been on the air with them. I thought about it very seriously.

But I can see how people would say, well, in effect...

Or if...I'm going...I'm speaking next month to the wine and spirits dealers. But we...all of us do.

HILTON: Of course. But just let me ask you this question. Are you compromised as a result of going to make a speech for Amway if, in fact, something comes up with Amway again, and you would get assigned to cover it?

WALLACE: No.

HILTON: Would you disqualify yourself?

WALLACE: Certainly not. I would not.

HILTON: But wouldn't that, perhaps, be seen by somebody else as a conflict of interest? You've taken their money.

WALLACE: It could be. It could be.

HILTON: We all have to be very careful....

WALLACE: Maybe I shouldn't do the Amway thing. It's conceivable I shouldn't do it.

Three things of predictable certainty happened in the ensuing months after my interview in July with Mike Wallace.

1) The discourse above was not included in the "Camera Shy" segment on *60 Minutes*.

2) What was included was my first comment above (in italics): *"We don't use news persons,"* and of course it was juxtaposed with film footage of Edwin Newman, clearly implying that I was fudging with Mike. (To repeat, purely for the record: Ed has never sat in that chair or interviewed any of my clients.)

In answering Mike's question, I thought I was remembering Mr. Sevareid's good advice to "... know your facts, have a sound case, and tell the simple truth."

But I was forgetting my own advice (see chapter 3) to avoid inquisitorial interviews unless subpoenaed, especially those which are truncated by a tape editor.

Oh, yes. I almost forgot the third thing. In the fall, Mike traveled to Grand Rapids, Michigan, and spoke to that Amway group for his regular fee (which is enormous).

chapter eighteen

Communications in a Crisis

It's a favorite story of mine and it's true, which makes it even better.

At a Texas oil refinery about 10 or 12 years ago, no tidbit of information was permitted to reach the press until it was Sanforized and okayed by a management committee, which met in general session every weekday morning at 10 o'clock.

One afternoon, the refinery manager left his post uncustomarily early to attend an important dinner that evening. For some reason he neglected to tell his secretary and staff about his plans and was incommunicado for several hours thereafter, a highly unusual state of affairs for a man ultimately responsible for megamillions of dollars of facilities.

Later that night the manager and his wife returned to their home after dinner just in time for the 10 o'clock news on television. The lead story, live by minicam from the refinery, showed the place on fire. In the background were muffled explosions and towers of flame. In front of the camera, with the conflagration as a backdrop, stood a public relations aide for the refinery. Pinned against a cyclone fence, he was surrounded by a throng of reporters, a cluster of microphones thrust in his face.

"What started the fire?" screamed a questioner over the din.

"What fire?" yelled the PR man.

On the next morning at 10 A.M., from makeshift quarters, the management committee made the appropriate declaration about the accident and issued a mimeographed release to the local news organizations.

Here we are skipping merrily through a book about press relations that harps incessantly about preparation, and all of a sudden an explosion occurs! Reporters and camera crews will be on the site momentarily in their radio-dispatched mobile units. Minicams and Betacams (small, battery-operated television cameras) and microwave hops will enable the TV people to transmit live from the scene. Now what?

Fundamentally the answer is threefold: (1) prepare to be unprepared, (2) stick to the facts that you know about personally; tell the straight truth, and (3) formulate your answers to who, what, when, where, why and how, which are the only questions you will likely be asked with a catastrophe still in progress.

"What started the fire?"

"Where?" (In what area of the plant?)

"When?" (At approximately what time?)

"Who was responsible?" (If anyone.) Or: "Who was in the immediate area of the explosion?" Or: "Who was injured?" (If anyone.)

"How did it happen? Why?" (Essentially we have come full circle. The latter two questions bear strong resemblance to the first one: "What started the fire?")

In responding on the spot to these and similar queries (all basic), please revert to tip #2 above, and don't speculate. Hearsay is a no-no, too. It is perfectly permissible in an emergency, if you don't know the answer, to say, "I don't know the answer." The alternative is to prove that you don't know, usually at length, which has the potential to compromise everyone and everything when the smoke finally clears. In the succeeding hours and days after a disaster, your mission is to add to the record of accurate information. You have flopped under fire if your subsequent time is otherwise spent attempting to mollify and retract.

Safety and compassion, not culpability and excuses, are the first priorities, and all-purpose statements like any of the following will play marvelously in the morning papers and on TV:

> Our prime interest is to control the present situation, and attend to anyone who is hurt.

The surrounding area is, or isn't, threatened, and the residents are advised to evacuate, or remain in their homes.

Let me explain, at least hastily, our internal investigative procedures for emergencies such as this.

We will make an interim and no doubt incomplete report of our findings to the press at noon tomorrow.

A final report will be issued when we're sure it's final—and correct.

"Prepare to be unprepared" is one of those goody-goody bromides, and at the same time it is goody-goody advice. Take a look around, preferably before the next eruption occurs, and think in terms of Murphy's Law: What can possibly go wrong here? Accidents and catastrophes come in the form of fires, explosions, emissions, and collapses, among others. Are you susceptible? The upshot can be injuries and fatalities. Is flooding a possibility, or health risks from toxic substances? What about heavy machinery and equipment? Crimes and intrusions are sometimes perpetrated (to use the police term).

Make the list as complete as you can, and then ask yourself the following questions: If anything happens, what will I (we) do first, second, third, fourth, and fifth? It's called contingency planning, which is preparation for "an event that may occur, but is not likely or intended; a possibility."

Among my clients are several hundred industrial companies and, after a few decades in this line of work, everything mentioned two paragraphs ago has occurred at least once in my personal experience. (No, I'm not jinxed. At least I don't think so.) For handling the press in the immediate aftermath, we finally set down a list of general guidelines: "Notes on crisis management—or how to prevent a second crisis with the press and other outsiders."

A few excerpts are germane.

1. The best crisis relations are based on the best press relations. And the best press relations are based on ties developed when neither the press needs the company nor the company needs the press. In other words, when there is no crisis.

2. A poor in-crisis performance, of course, puts a company at point-zero, or worse. Bonds with the press are broken, and the word goes out that "these people aren't to be trusted." But good crisis management as a follow-up to good noncrisis press relations cements the ties already in place.

3. Spokespeople must be knowledgeable. A company should select people with expertise concerning matters about which the press may be interested, people who have the background to draw upon information that is second nature to them.

4. But it's also important to have as liaisons with the press people who understand reporters, people with the personality and temperment that turn journalists on rather than off.

   Attitude is important: A welcoming attitude, an attitude of helpfulness, an attitude of openness, an attitude of giving, an attitude of concern.

5. Newspaper reporters can be expected to need and use more information than their counterparts in television. They're interested in basic facts for today's editions, and information on background and the implications for tomorrow's papers. Because they have more time, they're likely to check out the facts (at least for all but the first edition).

6. Broadcast journalists will want less and check back less. They'll be in more of a hurry and will seek updates, particularly if they work on the radio side where news goes out on the hour or quicker.

7. All journalists will seek accounts of the event, interviews with the persons involved (as well as company representatives), and opportunities to photograph the scene.

8. All journalists (good ones, persistent ones) will get their stories, correct or not, with the cooperation of management or not.

9. Reporters provide few surprises in crisis situations. They just want the basic information, plus human interest. They want it easily and quickly.

   That means the person who speaks for the company should get clear in his or her mind what happened, where it happened, when it happened, to whom it happened, why it happened, and how it happened. It is as simple as that.

10. When it comes to sources who help and sources who hinder, a journalist's memory becomes the proverbial elephant's. His or her story is likely to reflect that help or hindrance, through nuances of coverage, and even through explicit mention of the cooperation received or the lack thereof.

11. It is hard for corporate people to win when they compete with the press, because the battle is always waged on the press's terms. It's easier for corporate people to win when they march in lockstep with the press, as best and as far as they can, because then it's not a battle. It becomes a collaboration, a group effort, depicting an event or situation. A company does better not being left out of the picture or the credits.

12. A crisis team should include a public relations representative at the facility, if there is one; a top management representative to make necessary decisions quickly; someone from the personnel department or industrial relations to keep employees informed, to supply information on affected employees, and to notify next of kin; a member of plant security to control the situation and communicate with the police and fire department; an operations or maintenance representative who understands emergency water connections, power lines, and blueprints; and a photographer to document the event. Also helpful are a medical staffer, particularly if OSHA and EPA matters are involved, and an expert to provide technically complex answers.

13. Brevity, specificity, and clarity should be the spokesperson's goals. Verbal agility helps. So does an ability to transform negative questions and a negative situation into as much of a positive as possible and to speak convincingly of the company's compassion and long-standing concern for the community's environment. Preparation helps, but the man or woman who speaks needs to be attuned to that sort of approach.

14. Much basic information can be forgotten under pressure. A fact sheet about the facility and its operations, prepared in advance, fills the gaps of memory.

15. Reporters need a place to work and to be briefed. Choosing a location (and an alternative location) ahead of crisis time is essential. It should be a place with phones, space, sufficient seating, and enough lights and electrical outlets to accommodate the broadcasters.

16. When it happens (get ready for another bromide)

    A. Be cool. (Practice makes perfect.)
    B. Team members should be sent to their posts immediately (and should be in touch with each other).
    C. The facts of the situation should be ascertained.
    D. A preliminary statement should be prepared.
    E. Company personnel and local government officials should be notified.
    F. The press should be called, then, on arrival, taken care of.
    G. Employees should be advised of the problem's extent— of the shutdown (or whatever)—and what the crisis will mean to them.

17. And when it's over, it ain't over (Yogi Berra notwithstanding). The crisis team continues to function as the prime source of information for insiders and outsiders. Investigators, union representatives, elected officials, and regulatory agencies will seek information. And even the fickle press, on to bigger and worse things, will need to be kept alert to developments.

18. A crisis is still a crisis, but at least the constituencies (in-house, in the community, in Washington, and so on) will not contribute to making it worse if the unexpected and the unwanted have been planned for.

In my experience, only the atypical chief executive can perform correctly under stress in the spokeman's role, and I have a theory about the reasons why. In most big businesses, especially at the top, the assistants closest to the senior officers erect protective cocoons around their leaders. Routinely they screen out all but the most important callers and problems, and make life as easy as possible for the chiefs of state. The bosses, as a consequence, are less accustomed than you are to dealing with adversity in personal encounters; they're less frequently challenged, especially when those challenges are aimed at their authority and power. For anyone accustomed to insulation, challenges are disproportionately unsettling, and that is why, when CEOs first encounter the press, many of them come off so badly.

If you can, keep the boss in the back room until the crisis has cooled. Tell him that's why he's paying you. Tell him General Eisenhower rarely visited the front. Tell him anything.

And if you *are* the boss, please take heed. Keep your head down!

chapter nineteen

L'Esprit
de l'Escalier

Except for chance encounters in a washroom or on the Staten Island Ferry, we have covered most of the situations where you might be cross-examined by reporters with the exception of three: (1) on the phone, (2) in your office or home, and (3) on the radio. Frequently they happen in combination. Office or home interviews are commonly conducted on the telephone, and sometimes on the radio, too. It isn't necessary in many instances to schlep to the local station, or to a radio outlet far distant, in order to make an appearance on the air. One night a few years ago, at the time of the Reagan–Mondale debates, I participated in six or seven radio programs from New York State to California between 7 P.M. and midnight, eastern time. I was barefoot, wearing jeans, unshaven, and sprawled on the floor in the dark in my company's Manhattan apartment. One station in Syracuse connected me with callers from Quebec and elsewhere in its coverage area, and our listeners surely included truckers on the run throughout the northeastern quadrant of the United States. I had the phone company to thank or blame for that experience and convenience.

Phone interviews with reporters from newspapers or radio stations are either the hardest or the easiest for me to pull off, and I owe you several hundred words to explain that apparent contradiction.

They're harder because they're more exhausting. I am easily distracted, especially by something visual, so I force myself to concentrate inordinately in an empty room with only the ceiling or my fingernails at which to stare. The exhaustion is intellectual, not physical, which I think is the most tiring kind. I sleep more soundly at night after sparring in a debate with a skilled adversary than I would after shoveling gravel for eight hours. Also, I don't like the phone in the first place, except for the tersest or most businesslike communications; it is a poor, but frequently necessary, substitute for the face-to-face encounter. I think I speak for a sizable portion of the American population, including neither of my daughters.

But a phone interview is easier for me, too, because I'm not completely reliant on my memory or quick wittedness (which occasionally elude me). Someone once said, "Plan your ad-libs in advance," which is not only a contradiction of terms, but exceedingly fine advice. For a phone interview, I not only plan ad-libs, I jot them down on slips of paper for easy reference, and the other guy is never the wiser. I sound more like a Fulbright scholar with the appropriate notes and reference materials strewn at hand on my desk or coffee table.

The French refer to l'esprit de l'escalier. Roughly translated it means that a killer rejoinder has finally occurred to you several hours after a provocation or insult, as you mount the staircase at home en route to beddy-bye for the night. At that point the squelch is completely useless, of course, because timing is everything in a debate or discussion. But on the phone with a list of those rejoinders at the ready, the moment is rarely lost.

Incidentally, I am a general advocate of written notes, and I'm not suggesting that you hide them either. On occasion, I even use notes on television. If the conversation is about repealing the 22ND Amendment to the U.S. Constitution (limiting U.S. presidents to two terms in office), I may not remember offhand that it was vindictively proposed on March 24TH, 1947 (after FDR's fourth election), and proclaimed on March 1ST, 1951. It exempted Harry Truman, but not by name. In that regard, its wording was the following: "This article shall not apply to any person holding the office of president when this article was proposed by the Congress, and shall not prevent any person who may be holding the office of president, or acting as president, during the term within which this article becomes operative from holding the office of president or acting as president during the remainder of such term" (no doubt written by a lawyer). Those particulars of fact, listed on a sheet of paper in a manila folder on my lap, might come in handy in a TV conversation about the amendment; they might establish me as a better authority on the topic than anyone else on the panel, and they might engender admiration or respect from the audience. "He did his homework," they might conclude. "I'll listen to him more closely," as opposed to the other blabbermouths.

If I can use notes in plain sight on a television program to advantage, you can do likewise on TV, and on the phone, and certainly in an office interview with a newspaper reporter.

You can also buy time in the latter situation. "Excuse me, Scoop," you can say. "Let me get my notes from the file." He has just delivered the coup de grace. You need a moment for thoughtful reflection before you counter-coup de grace, a moment to mount that mental staircase, a luxury of precious time not available to you on television and radio. "I'll be right back," you tell him.

It matters not if you return in two minutes without a folder in your hand, saying "I'm sorry. The papers I wanted must be misplaced." It only matters that two minutes have been gained for purposes of composure, both the emotional and the intellectual kind. (If you use this ploy, please promise to return, at least eventually. This is no time to go home or out to lunch, unless you know of a place not covered by extradition agreements.)

Also in the office, you needn't solo like you do in most instances on TV and radio. If the newspaperman's topic is metallurgy, it's your call (not his) if you want your best metallurgist to be present, or your chief of staff, your plant manager, or even your lawyer.

When your remarks in an office interview are excerpted for later broadcast or recounted by a newspaper or magazine writer, accuracy and context may be a concern of yours (over which you exercise little or no control). People often complain in the after-math of interviews that they were misquoted or quoted out of context, and frequently they are, sometimes due to malice on the part of reporters, most times due to sloppiness. People sometimes misspeak, too. ("Damn it! You quoted what I *said*, not what I *meant!*") It's handy in those cases to have a record of the conversation in the form of a transcript, which necessitates that an audio tape be made during the interview itself. That's entirely your right, especially in your own home or office, and it's also advised if the encounter is expected to be confrontational or adversative.

Have the tape transcribed as soon as possible. There are transcription services in virtually every city, but any dummy can start and stop an audio tape and transfer its content to paper. (First, Mike said this: "Quote." Then Jack said that: "Quote." And so on. Just be sure as you review the written transcript and check it against the tape recording that everyone has been quoted carefully and faithfully. Usually that requires some revising of the first-draft and blue-penciling.)

This ploy and protection does one more thing for you in addition to providing a record, if necessary, for later use. It serves notice on the reporter in an inoffensive and largely unspoken way that accuracy will count in his or her final grade. His note taking may become more scrupulous and conscientious; he may check back with you about a comment before he publishes it, if only because he knows you're in possession of that goddamn tape, which you can duplicate and forward at any later date to his boss, a grand jury, or the trial judge.

I've never done it, but it also occurs to me that you might even influence the editorial process if you mail an extra copy of the typewritten transcript to the reporter in advance of publication or broadcast. If he knows that you know what you said in reponse to questions #5 and #16, he is less likely to transpose those answers.

QUESTION #5: "Did you win a Rhodes scholarship in college?"

ANSWER: "Yes, I did."

QUESTION #16: "Did you kidnap the Lindbergh baby?"
ANSWER: "No, I didn't."

That example is ludicrous, but you get my drift.

Notwithstanding the miracle of telephonic communications at home or work, there will be occasions for schlepping to the local radio outlet for an interview on the air, and let me take a moment right here to prepare you for a considerable shock. Once through the reception area, the place will remind you of a warehouse, which is an impression you don't get by listening to the station. Inevitably the coffee which you'll be offered in a paper container will be sludge brewed earlier in the day, sometimes earlier in the week. In the main, let's be charitable, personnel will be casually dressed. (The current fashions are New Bohemia and *Miami Vice*, although current fashions are prone to change without notice. A few radio engineers with whom I worked in my early career never changed their garb, even day-to-day or week-to-week. It's unpredictable.)

The announcer or host who draws the assignment to interview you may be casually dressed, too, perhaps in something you would deem appropriate for raking leaves or cleaning out the garage. This may be a man whom you've heard on the radio. Maybe you pictured him in a three-piece suit, or even a tuxedo at night. On the radio, he is stentorian or dulcet. In person he is pockmarked and five feet-three, or six feet-five and 315 pounds. He may be unshaven, too. (When you leave, you will be motivated to shower and change clothes. You may be inclined to burn your clothes.)

The studio will be cramped and littered, or it may be a spacious room (still littered) in which old furniture, rugs, and filing cabinets also are stored. It will be dimly lit, or harshly lit. There is no middle ground. At the console behind a window in the adjoining room, an overweight engineer with lascivious eyes will be wolfing a deli sandwich and slurping coffee. You will appreciate the sturdy glass that separates you.

Your job in the interview is to completely disregard everything that I've said in the last three paragraphs. You will be heard on the air by thousands or millions of respectable people in the audience for whom the illusions about this particular station are intact. It sounds polished and professional to them. (One of my wisest radio mentors once described that medium as "the theater of the ear." What you see on the inside doesn't count.)

The announcer will ask you questions, some of them inane, and you will reply, using notes if you choose. (Incidentally, your announcer won't be called an announcer because that's old-fashioned and largely inaccurate. In the so-called golden age of radio in the 1930s and 1940s, announcers actually announced. Later they learned to talk more normally and conversationally on the radio, so it follows that today's announcers are called personalities or hosts. In newsrooms, they're called reporters or correspondents.)

The audience is still that amorphous group, not present and unseen, in uncounted homes. It isn't that slovenly, distracted guy across the table from you.

When this book is published, I expect to be invited to talk about it on the radio. That is every author's fervent hope and wish, because prospective buyers find out about the availability of books by listening to prattle on the radio (and, of course, on television, too). For that reason I have withheld my comments about typical station operations until chapter 19. It is my estimation (and here I concur with William F. Buckley, Jr.) that only a few of my engineering friends for the last 30 years have gotten to the 19TH chapter of any book if it isn't a technical manual. As a result, I still expect my reception at stations to be hospitable. (In other words, this is a test.)

Watch the clock. It will be visible somewhere in the studio, and you are advised to keep track of the allotted time as you and your host converse. If the interview is slated for 12:05 to 12:30, don't assume that 25 minutes are available for the latest of your triumphant and widely acclaimed Tocqueville lectures. In the first place, you will be interrupted once, twice, or three times by clusters of short commercial announcements and station promos. The host will interrupt you in midsentence if necessary, saying, "Hold that thought. We'll pick it up in a minute," or words to that effect. (Most times he won't remember to pick it up in a minute, so the opportunity has been lost for you to score that telling point on the previous topic when the program resumes. Coming back on the air after the detergent and pantyhose have been boosted, the host is likely to say, "Shifting gears altogether, I'd like to ask you. . . .") Sometimes, in interrupting you, the host will say, "More about that after this," which has always been a favorite of mine.

If two of those commercial and promotional minutes are saved for the end of the program, you'll be off at 12:28, not 12:30. Let's say two interruptions of 90 seconds each are scheduled somewhere between 12:05 and 12:28. Your 25 minutes is already reduced to 20 minutes in three blocks of conversation averaging 6 minutes and 40 seconds per segment.

Also, let's say that you and he or she approximately share the available time on an equal basis, which is not uncommon. Your time to hold forth is thusly reduced to three minutes and 20 seconds per segment. But wait! In each segment you will be called upon to answer six questions. (I'm guessing.) If you apportion the time equally, which, of course, you won't, each answer is destined for 30 seconds, which is approximately 85 words for me.

> Eighty-five words (spelled out as "eighty-five" instead of using numerals), if we set them in cold type and printed them on the page which you are currently reading, are fewer words by an actual count of one hundred eighty-one than Abraham Lincoln needed for the Gettysburg Address—or twenty-six less than were required to compose the twenty-third Psalm—and in total would very closely resemble this indented paragraph, for which I need only seven more words in order to complete.

Without forethought and preparation, that may be an insufficient number of words to explain the coefficient of haze, although it's probably adequate to describe William ("The Refrigerator") Perry.

As I have been saying off and on for 19 chapters (largely unbeknownst to the engineers behind the glass) get to your point sooner rather than later, lest the host be compelled (in the middle of your most important speech) to intone that "the last 25 minutes have been a fascinating out of body experience and a slice of life, elapsing all too quickly, but the only dictator to whom we bow on Talk Radio 85 is the clock. Please drop in again whenever you're visiting in the vicinity of Torrington, Wyoming—the land of the free and the home of the brave."

About that perfunctory invitation: if you were a socko guest, he really means it.

chapter twenty
Small Talk

Some of the best lessons are the simplest, and the best language is likewise. (Take for instance the 22ND Amendment. It really says: except for the person or persons who hold the job while this travesty of a bill is being considered and approved or refused, no one else can be elected to the U.S. presidency more than twice.)

Meeting the press on television or radio is to be seen and heard by a legion of folks in thousands or millions of households who aren't conversant with your jargon. Make it easy for them to understand you. Don't talk about a maldistribution of primary health care deliverers if you simply mean there's a shortage of family doctors in the rural areas. If you're talking about a shovel, don't gurgle aloud about a portable, manually operated earth relocator.

This isn't to suggest that you patronize people or indulge in baby talk. If a fancy word is best use it, and find a way to define it for the rest of us. But it's odds-on that something simpler is just as expressive and correct, and far more meaningful to the mass audience.

Naturally, the worst offenders in this connection are writing constitutional amendments and otherwise bollixing the nation's business in Washington, D.C. (where Richard Nixon labored repeatedly to "make one thing perfectly clear," and finally he succeeded). One day in *The Federal Register*, I came across the following passage, written in a lexicon known locally as bureaucratese. (The translation will follow, but no fair peeking.).

We respectfully petition, request, and entreat that due and adequate provision be made, this day and the date hereinafter subscribed, for the satisfying of these petitioners' nutritional requirements and for the organizing of such methods of allocation and distribution as may be deemed necessary and proper to assure the reception by and for said petitioners of such quantities of baked cereal products as shall, in the judgment of the aforesaid petitioners, constitute a sufficient supply thereof.

King James said it better: "Give us this day our daily bread."

I photocopied that *Register* page and sent it to a friend of mine, now deceased. A week later in the mail, I received a short essay in return. Its title was "small talk," with a small "s" and "t," like e.e. cummings used to do it.

No law says you have to use big words when you write or talk.

Most small words can say all you want to say. It may take some time to find them, but it's worth it.

Some small words are rich with just the right feel, the right taste; the cold, deep dark of night; the hot, salt sting of tears.

Small words can be crisp, brief, terse—to the point.

They can catch great ideas and hold them up, like rare stones in rings of gold, or joy in the eyes of a child.

Small words move with ease where big words stand still and get in the way of what you want to say.

Have I made my point?

chapter twenty-one
The Political Equivalent

Finally, the last chapter! It appears for two purposes.

First, I wanted to save some vital and juicy advice, heretofore unmentioned, for the end of the book to foreclose a possible conclusion on your part that I haven't said anything new since page 75.

Secondly, most publishers think all readers are morons so they want everything regurgitated, as if you've forgotten what came before or can't glance back at it. (This publisher, of course, is the exception.)

My strategy here is to mix those things together (something old, something new, nothing borrowed without attribution and permission), hoping that you won't stop reading before I stop writing. (Let me know if it's successful. Cards and letters are invited at 230 Park Avenue, New York City 10169. No packages, please. We've been soaking them since the last bomb scare.)

Earlier I stated some reasons why you might be interested in HOW TO MEET THE PRESS. Here they are again, plus a few more:

- You have achieved, or intend to achieve, a degree of prominence or notoriety in your chosen field, and the press has noticed you, or shortly will. Andy Warhol was right. Almost every one of us in this era of mass and instantaneous communications is probably destined to be famous for at least 15 minutes.

- Maybe you're a complete greenie about press relations while at the same time you are highly accomplished and highly paid as something else. Nonetheless, you are largely or wholly inexperienced with nosey reporters.
- Because of the above-mentioned accomplishments and rank, you are about to become, or hope to become, newsworthy, perhaps "overnight". (Except when referring to the dark period between sunset and sunrise, I always put that word in quotes because most "overnight" sensations in American society have been working on it for approximately twenty years.)
- If you have achieved newsworthiness, or if that's your plan, you also have something to tell us, and we the people will listen and be interested. You have something to explain, refute, sell, or relate. (Fill in your favorite verb.) You hope to be convincing and persuasive; to marshal support; or to garner admiration, respect, and acclaim. (Leftover verbs or nouns go here.)
- Maybe you have something to hide or deny, which is why the press noticed you in the first place. (If true, keep reading as fast as you can and don't answer the phone.)
- If none of the above is apt, why the hell are you still here? Perhaps you're mainly curious in a masochistic way about the press and how it operates. Have you got some time to kill?

Somewhere above, I may have ascribed a motivation (or compunction) of yours. At the same time, I've also described every political candidate, municipal, federal, and anything in between or on the fringes, ever known. And although you may not be a prospect for president of the United States (or perhaps you are) it's useful and instructive for us to glean some final lessons from the political establishment; their aims and yours are akin in many respects. No other group relies more fervently on press notice and favor.

For example, in perusing my previous writings and observations about national elections (articles and books, TV and radio essays) it occurs to me at this juncture that the whole collection might be titled *How to Meet the Press.* Fundamentally, that's what a campaign is all about: using the press as a conduit for meeting the people. In one of my daily commentaries for the North American Radio and Television Alliance, I once said, "Eighty million Americans voted for president in 1980. A fraction of that total ever saw the candidates in person. Most of us get most of our news and information from television, and we believe it. For a political candidate, there's nothing more important than television."

Accordingly, another New York-based media adviser by the name of Tony Schwartz once said on television, "A candidate on the most crowded street corner in the world, shaking hands with a different person every 10 seconds, couldn't shake hands in a whole campaign with a fraction of the people who see one commercial, where the same candidate can talk to them in their own homes directly. . . ."

As a result, Schwartz contends, so-called public speaking is anachronistic. Private speaking, on television, makes the difference, he says.

Inhibitions in the Age of Exhibition

Unfortunately for the two of them, Walter Mondale and Gary Hart never mastered private speaking on television in 1984, as Mr. Mondale acknowledged after Election Day. Neither man used the medium up close and personally. Heritage may have been a factor. Mondale and Hart were raised by no-nonsense disciplinarians and religious fundamentalists. Both came to public life surrounded by walls of reserve, which neither could scale. Nor could the voters peek in.

The rote impressions of Gary Hart were cool or aloof. It isn't true, he kept insisting. He was shy, he said, reticent and uneasy with people. But on television, he seemed aloof and distant, even "strange," said Ken Auletta, one of my fellow commentators on WCBS. (Appearances count for more than reality on television.)

In childhood, Walter Mondale was taught the right stuff by his father, which was to be reserved, formal, and modest in public; to have good manners; to wear a white shirt and dress nicely; to keep his hair neatly cropped and parted; and mostly to resist revealing himself. Arriving at the office on his first day as Minnesota's Attorney General, Mr. Mondale remarked to a friend, "I'm never going to smile in public." He felt that no expression was his best expression and no emotion his best posture. Years later as a U.S. Senator, one of his colleagues, Fred Harris, once said, "Mondale worries about a person being too open like Hubert Humphrey. If he (Mondale) shows his emotions, he feels it might get him in trouble."

Those inhibitions and reservations were seemingly ingrained, perhaps as a consequence of their upbringings. But because of television, we're now living in an age of exhibition in America, not to mention expostulation.

If you subscribe to my contention that style is predominant over substance on TV, you also may conclude that personality (a politician's or anybody else's) is central to the prospect for one's success. Some of them play better than others, in Peoria and elsewhere. (Some of them play strangely or reservedly.)

I was asked in '84 what I might have done to assist Mondale in that connection. (I wasn't asked by him, however. He was coached by a labor lawyer for the TV debates!) At the time I happened to be immersed in a newspaper article about Mr. Mondale's warmth and appeal in private settings with a close circle of friends. Let it be seen in public, I said. Why not, if it's really him? To do otherwise on TV is to be untrue in the strictest sense. To be untrue is to be disingenuous, which can be interpreted as insincere.

In Mondale's view, judging from his subsequent remarks, it was a badge of honor to disdain the advice of a television consultant in 1984. "What you see is what you get," he said in a July speech at Elmore, Minnesota (his childhood home). Later he bragged about resisting "the Hollywood make-over," as he put it. But a make-over is the *opposite* of what I would have attempted. Rule #1 in this book is *be yourself,* Fritz.

Even if a dictionary is handy, don't bother looking up the definition of *sincere.* Here it is: "not feigned or affected; true. Presenting no false appearances; not hypocritical; honest. Pure; unadulterated." (Few of us are advised to go that far in public.) Years ago I remember saying the following to another politician in a coaching session. I said it jocularly, but I said it nevertheless: "Sincerity is everything on television. Once you learn to fake that, you've got it made."

Where's the Beef?

All sorts of personalities work like a charm on TV except the stoic and restrained. And even if your personality glows like a 10-watt bulb, you can still be interesting if you strive to be provocative. That's my goal as a television and radio essayist, for example. Like the Missouri mule, an audience's attention must first be won before anything else can be accomplished. One day in a probably vain attempt to explain Ronald Reagan's theory of trickledown economics, I said, "When David Rockefeller is doing really well financially, some of it eventually trickles down to Jay Rockefeller."

Remarking on WCBS about the eventual Democratic nominee in 1984, I said, "This man has made considerable progress in his political career. Now he's a major candidate for president of the United States. Ten years ago, most people thought Mondale was a suburb of Los Angeles."

About Senator Hart: "He's entirely too intense and serious and, as a result, he comes across aloof and arrogant on television. I think he had charisma as a child, but it's cleared up."

About John Glenn: "A la FDR, he once tried a 'fireside speech' on television. The fire went out."

About George McGovern in 1984: "When he declared his candidacy, I wasn't sure if he was running for president or bucking for a spot on the endangered species list."

Don't misunderstand. You're aiming for memorability and notice, but you needn't hire Dick Cavett or Robert Orben to write one liners. A well-turned phrase, a well-drawn analogy, or a vivid word picture will enhance your attractiveness to the press. To use a hackneyed expression, they're looking for quotable quotes to enliven their articles and programs. As Jim Loughman mentioned in a previous chapter: "Dare to be different."

The Evening Stars

The aforementioned media adviser, Tony Schwartz, referred to the power of TV commercials. But perhaps you don't have a vast budget to advance your cause or yourself. Don't despair.

"The value of paid media has declined," said Frank Mankiewicz in 1984. "The value, use, and instruction the electorate gets from 'free media' is infinitely more important, and more available, than at any time in the past."

Mr. Mankiewicz worked as a campaign helper for Gary Hart in 1984, although he figured more prominently in a similar capacity for Bobby Kennedy in 1968. Said Senator Kennedy at that time: "I'd rather have a half-minute on the evening television news than a full column in every edition of the next day's newspapers."

Getting 30 seconds on the nightly news is easier if the most pictorial of a day's campaign events is scheduled in the morning hours. TV crews in the field need time to edit and assemble their videotapes (for transmission by satellite to New York, where most of the network programs originate). From a toxic waste site in Alabama, a fiery speech at 10 A.M. is a cinch for the 7 o'clock news. The same speech after lunch is iffy.

Secondly, the medium of television is *show me* more than tell me. Easily as important as what a person says is where he says it, preferably in the foreground of a colorful and dramatic scene. The concluding exclamation of a speech may be excerpted and used on the nightly newscasts. Punctuated by a fanfare from the marching band, a simultaneous ascending of helium-filled balloons, and the crowd in tumult, it definitely will.[1]

You are highly attuned to press slang if photo opportunity is a familiar expression, and you, too, should be considering pictures to enhance your messages. As I mentioned before, some of our TV jargon is borrowed from newspapers and the printed press. Photo opportunity is another example. Before the advent of television, still photographers would shoot pictures of the principals for a minute or two before the likes of Franklin Roosevelt and Winston Churchill secluded themselves to decide the fate of humanity. It was an opportunity to make a photo of prominent public figures, and inevitably those photos of the President and the Prime Minister; smiling, shaking hands, making small talk, would appear on the front pages of the next day's papers. Then came the electronic age of journalism (cameras, microphones, videotape recorders), and now a photo op (for short) encompasses more than still pictures (although we still haven't thought up a new name). Almost every Saturday morning the President of the United States crosses the White House lawn to board a helicopter for Camp David, during which passage the press corps shouts questions and the President sometimes shouts back. That, too, is a photo opportunity, as are most presidential appearances.

The Gipper

Example: In June of 1984, a CBS commentator (not me) observed that the Democratic primary contenders would be

---

[1] Pardon the diversion, but speeches are written to be spoken aloud, not read silently. That's why a tongue twister like "the concluding exclamation" would be excised from a text before delivery. On paper that phrase may seem benign, but it's difficult to articulate. For me, it's almost impossible. Why stumble? Let's make it "a big finish."

eclipsed on TV by pictures of Ronald Reagan's grand tour. Included on the President's itinerary were Buckingham Palace, the Economic Summit in London, and a commemoration of D-Day in Normandy—fabulous pictures all! Partisanship was implied by the commentator, as if Eisenhower and the Allies had planned their invasion to screw Walter Mondale 40 years later. (At least that's what I inferred.)

The European trip in '84, in addition to the business which may have been transacted, was an extended photo opportunity for the President. Another occurred a month earlier on Mr. Reagan's imperial visit to China. At that time, I took note of it on the air:

> We're witnessing a dazzling example of a presidential campaign staged for American television with the President on the high road to China and Alaska for a six-day "photo opportunity."
>
> You've heard that phrase before, and we're seeing what it means in practice, courtesy of a skilled White House staff. They refer to TV pictures in scenic and dramatic settings with Mr. Reagan prominently in the foreground as "high profile presidential visuals."
>
> They considerably control the press, too. We're obliged to follow along in the wake of the leader of the Free World on the chance that something important may transpire. But the events are planned by them. Our access to the principals is limited or prevented. Our cameras are set up on their platforms, and we mostly record speeches and ceremonies which they've written and choreographed.
>
> So much for the pervasive power of the press.
>
> It's been a masterful performance, and we'll see more of the same next month—at the Economic Summit, and especially June 6TH on the beaches at Normandy for the 40TH anniversary of D-Day. I wouldn't be altogether startled to see the President wading ashore from an LST—provided it happens in front of network television cameras.
>
> That's what a so-called "photo opportunity" is all about.
>
> It also demonstrates the awesomeness of incumbency. While Fritz Mondale was campaigning at a bowling alley in Amarillo, Texas,

Mr. Reagan has been appearing "presidential" at the Great Wall of China in picture postcards for television—thanks to a trailing press corps of 300 correspondents and technicians.

All of that is lofty, and I don't want to lose anyone in the traces. Basically there are three lessons here, which are applicable to you.

First, traipsing with the First Family to Europe or Asia isn't the only way to command press attention (although it works every time, so be alert for the opportunity). To entice television coverage, the point is to dramatize your message or appeal. Wreck a tenement to launch an urban renewal program and the cameras will attend. Feed the hungry masses with fishes and loaves. Think events, not pronouncements.

Second, the infamous Michael Deaver played the Busby Berkeley role as producer and picture man for President Reagan until 1985, but he doesn't own visual thinking. Street festivals (ethnic costumes, exotic foods, entertainment) are standard fare on TV news.* Children and pets are irresistible, as are antiques, rallies, concerts, parades, Rube Goldberg inventions, and panoramic vistas at sunset (with a string quartet in the foreground). Like Deaver, think pictures, not palaver.

---

* On the upcoming events blotter at one of New York's television stations were the following entries for an 80-day period in 1986: Ecuadorian Festival (August 10), Dominican Day Parade (ditto), Fiesta Folklorica (August 24), West Indian-American Day Carnival (August 28), Queens Ethnic Music and Dance Festival (September 6), Great Irish Fair (September 6-7), One-World Festival (ditto), Feast of the Giglio (September 7), Brazilian Independence Day Festival (ditto), Ganesh Chathurthi Celebrations (ditto), Feast of San Gennaro (September 11-21), Afro-American Day Parade (September 14), Choo Seok: Korean Harvest Festival (ditto), Steuben Day Parade (September 20), Korean Day Parade (October 4), Pulaski Day Parade (October 5), Columbus Day Parade (October 11), Hispanic-American Day Parade (October 12) and the Tibetan Harvest Festival (October 19). In the absence of more compelling news on any of the above-mentioned dates, it's likely that snatches of these indulgences were seen on television by New York audiences. It's likelier still that camera crews and reporters were dispatched to the various sites whether or not the footage ever saw the light of day.

177

Third, pay heed to Frank Mankiewicz concerning "free media." Every TV and radio station in your community has at least one program on its daily or weekly schedule where you might appear if your cause is just (maybe otherwise, too).

Hope and Fear

Let us depart this vale on a strategic note of some importance dealing with the substance of your message for the public. It will gain reception and favor if it's intuitive. Immediate cognition will result. Or it will be rejected or ignored if it seems counter-intuitive, if somehow it doesn't jibe. This explains why opinion polling has become an integral part of American politics. Candidates seek first to determine the moods and positions of the populace before they strike their campaign stances, determining in advance what the people already believe or are prepared to believe. Those beliefs can be evoked and intensified, usually resulting in a cascade of votes for the little dickens who pulls it off.

For instance, the nation was brimming with confidence in the third quarter of 1984. (Remember the Summer Olympics in Los Angeles, the invasion of Grenada, a robust and recovering economy?) In September, a cover story in *Time* magazine was about "America's Upbeat Mood."

But in the first of Walter Mondale's television commercials after the Democratic convention, we saw a roller coaster, struggling up the tracks and hurtling downward, as the announcer said, "(The U.S. economy is) moving up on a mountain of debt and record Reagan deficits... that will drive interest rates up... and slow the economy down...."

Central message: Fear.

Meanwhile over at 79 Wistful Vista the Reagan camp had somehow resurrected Norman Rockwell ("It's Morning in America") evoking feelings of good will and patriotism with their commercials.

Central message: Hope.

178

Mr. Mondale's pitch seemed dissonant at the time. When I first saw it, the stock market was going bonkers; one day it traded a record 236,000,000 shares in what was termed a "buying panic." The Dow skyrocketed 36 points in a single session. Inflation was minuscule, employment was up, and brokers were chorusing in the papers that interest rates would soon decline, which they did for the rest of that year.

After November 6th, the final score was tallied by the U.S. Electoral College.

Hope: 525 votes. Fear: 13.

Months later on *Meet the Press* on NBC, Mr. Mondale reflected on the fact that his campaign hadn't conveyed his messages in the right ways. Except for people in the District of Columbia and Minnesota, the former Vice President hadn't played harmonious music for his fellow citizens.

Bullishness, not bearishness, seemed to be indicated in view of "America's Upbeat Mood," and that might have been accomplished by the Democrats without compromising their convictions.

Things can be better is the flip side of things might get worse.

The difference between the two was demonstrated in 1963 at the Washington Monument, where Martin Luther King's message for America was inspirational, not threatening or destructive. Repeatedly he said in his speech: "I have a dream." It was a dream of better things and better times.

In that spirit I offer a last kernel of friendly advice about your messages, reminding you of a song lyric written decades ago by the late Johnny Mercer: "Accentuate the positive, eliminate the negative, latch on to the affirmative, and don't mess with Mr. In-Between."

EPILOGUE

I planned to sub-title this book "a guerrilla guide," but a friend of mine in publishing circles counseled otherwise. It was his concern that you might be offended by that flammable word—"guerrilla"—which also (and admittedly) has odious and sinister overtones. I conceded at the last minute—a decision I still second-guess—and we finally settled on a tamer (and somewhat blander) sub-title: *A Survival Guide*.

However, unless you make it a habit of reading books backwards, you have discerned from the last 21 chapters that "survival" in press interviews isn't one of my main aspirations for you or anyone else. Instead, I gravitate to words like *accomplishment* and *success*. Here's another example of my reasons why.

In a workshop session a few years ago with the chairman of a major U.S. industrial company, my client "survived" an encounter on closed-circuit television with a trio of interrogators. That is to say he was still breathing afterwards—although shallowly and more quickly than before.

At one point in the interview, he was asked the following question: "Don't you agree that your company's diversification program in recent years has been monumentally stupid?"

It was early in our day, and my untutored client took serious issue in his response with the word "monumentally." He didn't agree at all, he said.

By contrast, my interviewers are anything but untutored—or compassionate. So for the next few minutes, they led him on a perilous jaunt through a long list of modifiers until the chairman finally settled on "moderately," as in "moderately stupid." En route, he rejected "colossally," "enormously," "prodigiously," and "unprecedentedly," among others. With each new word, my panel was afforded an opportunity to relate yet another blunder or example of stupidity on the company's part. Among those mentioned were "the real estate swindle" and the "record club hustle." But the chairman was so obsessed with substituting a better word for "monumentally" that he let those charges pass, or never really heard them until he and I reviewed the tape.

The two of us had a mirthful session after the interview ended. Mainly it was mirthful for him because the *only* copy of that cassette was destined for cold storage in his possession.

But now a thought occurs. If my present consternation about sub-titles had arisen at the time, I might have asked my client which book he would seek before his next TV appearance: a survival guide or a guerrilla guide?

Minus the odious and sinister connotations, I like the word "guerrilla"—it fits my line of work—because of how it's defined in the dictionary. A guerrilla, it says, is "a member of the military forces of a patriotic or revolutionary movement that seeks to immobilize and isolate the superior forces of an occupying enemy...."

It's true that I've always resisted the "warfare" inferences when it comes to press encounters because most interviews with reporters aren't wars, and I don't want them perceived that way by an audience. (Let's call them "jousts" instead—only the most difficult ones, that is.) But if "the superior forces of an occupying enemy" doesn't describe Sam Donaldson on the set of a David Brinkley show, he's changed a lot since last Sunday morning.

A couple of Donaldson's fellow panelists for the bull sessions in the last quarter-hour of the Brinkley program are clients of mine, and they strive each week to get a word in edgewise—or preferably a whole and cogent thought. Frequently, they succeed because we have devised tactics and strategies to (at times) "immobilize" and (mostly) "isolate" their conversational counterpart. These days, Sam's verbal geysers don't always emit unchecked or unchallenged, have you noticed?

A few years ago, I wrote an introductory chapter for another book. That treatise was called "The Rise of the Guerrillas," which I still think is more arresting than "The Rise of the Survivors." Vis-a-vis television, I was trying to start a minor movement in America on several fronts. The essay bears remembering, I think, with a few revisions and updatings.

In the beginning (not a bad place to start), when people first learned to talk, spreading the news was a simple matter of relating the day's events in front of a communal campfire. When Og played up his role in the hunt a bit beyond tolerance, Uk had his say at the evening fire, and if it took a bump on the head for Og to admit his exaggerations, well, a precursor of the fairness doctrine had its way of setting the record straight even then.

Tens of thousands of years later, the situation is much the same, except that newsmakers talk from a box in the living room (where they can't be bopped, although they can be refuted) and the fire remains in the furnace where it belongs, or flickers in a fireplace. Between the beginning and now, keeping an eye on important events became more difficult. The printing press eased matters, but the development of civilization around the world revised the "need to know" concept. For a while, if a person knew what was going on in his particular village, it was enough. Then if he knew what was going on in his kingdom, his region, or even on his continent, that was enough, too.

Now the whole village is a pretty big place to keep track of. No one person can keep up with the news without help. It's a function that has to be delegated to someone else, to someone we can trust to sift through the tens of thousands of books, thousands of magazines, the miles of reports and wire service stories, the endless hours of conversations with powerful and wise and absurd news shapers to get at the absolutely important facts and trends we need to know about to make it through another day.

That "someone" we trust the most is a mysterious entity called "the media," frequently used in a singular sense, as if it really "is" a person. Within that media structure is the medium of television, for instance. There are a number of networks, and within each network there are affiliates. Within each affiliate, which is a TV station to most people, there are individual news and information shows, run by people of varying talents and capabilities who must decide every day what goes in the line-up for broadcast. In the end, although this is not a comfortable thing for any of these people to acknowledge, they often don't know a hell of a lot more about what the audience wants or needs than the audience, sitting in front of its living room box, does.

Like the audience at home, they are dependent on *their* media—the network news structure, the wire services, government and corporate bodies—all of them populated with individuals who have different ideas about what the client at home needs to know.

What the media people *do* know, however, is what to do with the tools of their trade. And just in case the medium they work for is lacking, they invite the audience to venture into other media for balance or embellishment. Television people, who right now work for the number one medium in the country, often advise their audiences to read newspapers for the "complete story." Newspapers and magazines operate on the assumption that they are bringing the second word on any subject—after television. And radio assumes its audience is fickle, turning elsewhere after 30 minutes or so, so they repeat everything at regular intervals. Knowing the tools of the trade, media people also know their limitations.

And very humanly, they work from strength. Over the past 20 years, the sophistication of the tools has increased so much that the flashy effects they can achieve outweigh the content they deliver. An untrained person venturing before the camera to tell his or her story can easily fall victim to the TV medium. And without telling it on television, that person may never get his or her story across to the audience. This dilemma brought the rise of the television guerrilla, who learned enough about the medium to use it for his own purposes. That is not as diabolic as it may seem. We send our children to school to learn to read and write so they can be informed and can communicate with others. But in an age of electronic communication, reading and writing aren't enough. You have to know how to see, and perhaps be seen, how to listen, and perhaps how to talk into a microphone.

These days, a guerrilla guide to television may be almost as important as learning to read, because Americans get more information from that living-room box than anywhere else. Television isn't always fair or truthful, as Fred Friendly has noted in this book's foreword. It doesn't always tell you what you need to know, and despite all the editorial replies and fairness provisions, mistakes are still made, either because people don't know how to correct them or because they don't know how to fight back.

Now, if reading through this book (despite my efforts to the contrary) has convinced you to run the other way every time you see a television camera approaching, you can nevertheless do your part to make the broadcast game two-sided. Every sport needs its fans as well as its players.

A professional fan who understands the fine points of a game and its rules can actually improve the quality of performance. Once you are familiar with some of the traditional plays of broadcasting, the game itself begins to look different. Even the Sunday morning news and information shows—*Face the Nation, Meet the Press*, and *This Week with David Brinkley*—take on a new fascination. It is on these forums over the course of a season that you will see examples of nearly every good and bad technique on the part of panelists and guests. Some of the questioners dote on loading their opening remarks. A show seldom passes without a round of what-if or an absent-party question volley. It becomes easy to sort out the guests who know what the game is about from the guests who dig themselves a hole and pull it in after them. The shows are leisurely enough in terms of pace to help a spectator spot every play, so it's a good idea to begin with them.

Once you have mastered these, you'll find it easy to apply what you have learned to the faster paced nightly newscasts, where the rankest amateurs appear. With practice you'll be able to tell when a story has been heavily chopped up, and when an interview has been sliced into one sensational quote. A knowledgeable viewer who can spot the tricks of the trade soon becomes skeptical about the accuracy and completeness of the information that does come through, and loses interest in certain kinds of programs, particularly those run by uninformed moderators who permit garrulous guests to take over. The dumb question begins to stand out as if amplified. The evasive answer no longer has the power to deceive. In short, you have become a professional member of the audience, able in numbers—by switching the channel selector or using the "off" button—to improve the quality of broadcast communication.

The pros don't watch television or react the way an average audience does. If you ever have an opportunity to see a network news program with a group of local broadcasters, you'll witness a really professional audience at work. Instead of reacting to what is contained in the broadcast, they speculate on why one piece was given so much prominence, and how another piece of film or tape made the show on such late notice. They will comment on the anchorman's show of emotion at a particular point.

They will be discussing the style of the show, more than its content, because they know that style determines a show's ultimate impact. How someone on a program reacts to a question is far more important to them than what he said. Did he fall for the carefully laid trap or didn't he? Who scored the most points, the interviewer or the subject? *This* important story never made the news because it couldn't be visualized. *That* person, who knows the most about the subject, will not be interviewed because he or she is terrified of television and refuses all invitations to appear. Television—the medium that gives most people most of their information about almost everything—presents a world that is, at best, less than the whole story and, at worst, grossly distorted.

Knowing that a gulf exists between the TV screen and reality is helpful, but it's not enough. Consuming the news and information product of television without a grain of salt is downright dangerous. But by knowing something of the television encounter and how it works, a spectator can avoid drawing the wrong conclusions more often than not. Eventually it may lead him or her to question the rules of the game more closely. A broadcast need not engineer confrontation to make a subject interesting. Conversely, television need not be dull to be accurate and fair. It needs only to make the odds even for everyone.

186

Whether that is accomplished through a massive guerrilla training program or by a change in the medium itself is a question to be resolved by broadcasters and their audiences, aided by informed guerrillas who accept the challenge of the medium and win battles as well as lose them.

The first step in this process may be bad for the broadcast media, because it increases the skepticism of the audience. But it will be good in the long run, because television, like other big businesses, suffers from what its customers (the audience) *don't* know far more than from what they *do* know. It suffers more from what they don't see on the screen than from what they do.

Pollster Burns Roper had some interesting observations on the process of communications in a 1975 speech to the Public Relations Society. A few excerpts follow:

As a nation, we have become surfeited with formal communications systems and messages. Nobody could possibly keep up with all the messages conveyed through our elaborate and extensive media complex. I think there is no question but what this profusion of formal communications has increased people's awareness of issues, problems, and abuses that years ago they were oblivious to. While I think this communications system has caused people to be more knowledgeable than they used to be, I think it has also had the unfortunate effect of causing people to *feel* more knowledgeable than, in fact, they are. It would be my further contention that, as formal communications messages have been substituted for face-to-face or one-to-one communication, believability of the messages that have been transmitted and received has declined.

When people can relate to an individual, they tend to pay more attention, and they tend to find what he says more believable than what an amorphous, abstract corporation or other entity says. This is not to say that they will fully agree with the individual, but it is to say that they will both listen and have respect for what they hear. There has developed a "them" complex. You will hear people say, "All television repairmen are a bunch of crooks." Usually, if you ask, "Is your TV repairman a crook?" people will tell you that he is not. "He" is an individual; "they" are a foreign group.

I think it is important for an organization or institution to defend itself. One might say with low credibility on the one hand and self-

187

serving statements on the other, it is futile to defend one's self. However, I would say that if *you* don't defend yourself, almost certainly no one else will. Moreover, a non-defense becomes a tacit admission of guilt. Because of the problem of low credibility as well as reasons of simple honesty, I would "reveal the warts" and "tell it like it is." To admit one's error tends to take all the steam out of potentially hostile opponents and, in the process, to impart a credibility to the individual or organization making the statement. [I would] also tell the story to the people who don't know it rather than to each other.

Mr. Roper was arguing in his remarks for more openness of communication between big business and the public, but his advice is sound for anyone who has a message to deliver. He does not say which medium this individual should speak through, or how these confessions of guilt should be made, but television would seem one of the obvious answers.

With television's ability to bring a viewer face to face with the President of the United States, the head of General Motors, or a convicted murderer on the way to prison, we know and experience more than we used to. But it only *seems* that way. Like the shadows on the wall in Plato's cave, the real story is still some distance away. The directions on how to get there should be somewhat clearer than they were before this book.

Electronic Literacy

At various times in human history, whole classes, whole sexes, and whole peoples have been denied access to the tools of communication. In many civilizations, the skill of reading has been confined to a few, whose special knowledge allowed them to rule without interference.

Literacy and access to knowledge available through print and books have caused more than one revolution. Print literacy for centuries has been a means for the powerless or poor to gain power and wealth by educating themselves in new skills or by acquiring basic knowledge. Within the memory of many Americans are the infamous literacy tests of the South, which effectively blocked black voters from the polls for many years.

But the electronic media have replaced print as the basic source of information in this country, and the ordinary person has been severely limited in the ability to get before a microphone and camera. In fact, even the extraordinary person has found it difficult to reach an electronic forum with regularity.

All of that has begun to change, however, as television in new forms has become accessible to vast numbers of Americans for purposes quite different from the news and entertainment mix we usually consume on the major networks. In many areas, cable television has already opened new outlets for broadcasters and viewers, and pay cable programming has widened the entertainment choices for those to whom it is available. Pay cable, such as Home Box Office, offers original concerts, performances, and movies recorded solely for cable customers, and the full capacity of cable television, where it exists, has opened the door to nearly anyone who can find his or her way to a studio where community-access programs are produced.

Videocassette recorders are opening a market for prerecorded videotaped programs whose potential would seem to be endless. The day has arrived when a company will produce a videotape program for the home recorder, sold to VCR users at a slight discount for one viewing and erasure.

There are communications satellites. Barely into adolescence as a technology, the satellites orbiting the earth are used to process long-distance telephone calls and to extend television signals to remote areas of the world. Countries and companies can contract with Comsat and the National Aeronautics and Space Administration to put satellites into precise orbits over a continent, giving instant multichannel access to television in the remotest and most desolate areas.

A television set in an unwired home in an ordinary U.S. market uses a mere fraction of the available channels. As cable and satellite systems proliferate, more and more of these channels will become available to a single set, multiplying the choices of programming and adding new voices to the electronic spectrum. One of the pioneers in this field is Ted Turner, who transmits local programming from Atlanta, and a 24-hour news service, to cable television subscribers around the country. Religious television networks operate the same way. Others are following almost weekly.

Satellites also have the potential of making the ordinary business meeting a relic. It is now possible to be hooked up for over-the-air transmission with a meeting room in another city. The efficiency of this system is irresistible, even if you consider only the hours saved in travel and the general wear and tear on participants. Combining such a linkage with existing telecopying systems even allows documents to change hands during the course of an electronic meeting. Eventually all companies and organizations of any size will have their own satellite channel or channels, their own transponders for direct communication to and from a satellite, and the peripheral cameras and telecopiers.

If you are 30 years old, in business or the professions, the chances of your avoiding an appearance on television in the next 20 years are approximately zero. The audience for your television show may be small—six colleagues in another city, 25 salesmen in the Dallas office, one director in each of 12 cities. But you will be on television.

For many people such appearances will become as routine as a face-to-face meeting. Some people will take advantage of the medium instinctively, but unfortunately many will not realize the subtle and dangerous differences between talking to a camera and talking face-to-face until it is too late.

When you are in a face-to-face meeting with a group of people around a conference table, you do not look at all of them at the same time. Your eyes are like a camera tracking from one to the other, or focused on a single speaker or a single participant. Your companions are doing the same; some may not be looking at anyone at all. But when you are in an electronic meeting with your participants lined up with equal prominence on a projection television screen in front of you, you will look at the scene differently. While you are watching the president make a key point you will also see that Charley over there looks bored. Your eyes are focused on the entire image, not on a single object. You are seeing more than you would ordinarily.

A camera—especially one that has closeup powers—changes the viewer's perception. If you were sitting in an ordinary room attentively watching a speaker, he or she would be at some physical distance from you, anywhere from six feet away across a desk to 20 feet away at the other end of the conference room. But a television camera in closeup can move that person's face to an electronic distance physically equivalent to a nose-to-nose encounter. If you were to speak to a person with your noses touching in a face-to-face meeting, you wouldn't see any more than you see when you kiss someone with your eyes wide open. When a television camera does the equivalent of that closeup, you get a perspective you can never have in real life. *It changes reality.* You see things in a person's face you never saw before. You get clues to the person's state of mind that would be hidden at ordinary physical distances. And because of this artificial perspective, participants in an electronic meeting can inadvertently send and receive signals that were never intended.

In recent years, business executives and aspirants to high political office have become aware of the need to have a good television presence. They have learned that if they don't use the medium, it will use them.

The need to understand television's quirks, the tricks it plays, and the changes in emphasis it makes is not exactly a national obsession. People are not clamoring for lessons in electronic literacy as their forebears clamored for the right to read. Not yet, anyhow. So far, only those who have suffered the damage television can wreak on an amateur understand the need for electronic literacy. And it may be that open access to electronic literacy may not come until ignorance has created a national disaster. Even now the ability of a trained television communicator to sway an audience to his opinion is a potential danger. As politicians fight more and more of their campaign battles on the TV airwaves, it becomes more and more important for the audience to be able to separate style from substance, to see the tricks of the trade for what they are.

Early in our reading years, we run across our first instance of a lie committed in print. It can be devastating to learn that these magic things called words can be used to deceive as well as to reveal, yet somehow we have become inured to the risks, because day after day we electronic illiterates allow a minority of literate electronic professionals to bend our opinions and shape our thoughts. The reins of the Federal Communications Commission are loose at best, and organized citizen protests are pretty much limited to sex and violence and the advertising aimed at children.

Perhaps we need to teach people how to watch. It is just as important for the audience to know the ins and outs of the medium as it is for a person appearing on television. If the public remains passive, we may recreate in modern-day terms the situation of the Middle Ages, when the monks kept their knowledge locked in the exclusive club of those who read Latin while the populace knew only what the keepers of knowledge wanted them to know.

Today we insist that our educated citizenry have a working knowledge of our language and its powers. When students show a decline in language skills, it is cause for national alarm. Yet not once in an ordinary person's education (except for those bound for the sanctity of employment in the electronic media) is there a course on how to appear on, or react to, television. At best, students get courses in public speaking, modestly evolved from the days when people orated without benefit of microphone—a far cry from what is needed. How does that equip them to deal intelligently with a presidential campaign debate on television?

Today's students, pouring out of high schools and colleges, have a far greater chance of conducting at least a portion of their important business in front of a camera than they do of publishing their words or orating before a large live audience. And for sure, they will spend as many hours devouring the product of television as they do at anything else, with the possible exception of sleeping.

Epilogue

Television as we know it has evolved from the theater and the movies, and therefore its show business quotient is high. But there are certain elements that make television work differently from its forebears, too. If enough people understood its nature and limitations, it would be possible to set down some true guidelines on how television should operate to help its audience learn and its practitioners communicate. Without that knowledgeable audience, however, television will continue to muddle along as a tool of the initiates.

My guerrilla movement is aimed at vastly increasing the number of sophisticated initiates on both sides of the cameras.

Index

197

Index